Brian Patten

Richard Braine

BRIAN PATTEN

WW

Brian
Patten

Linda Cookson

WITHDRAWN

Northcote House
in association with
The British Council

© Copyright 1997 by Linda Cookson

First published in 1997 by Northcote House Publishers Ltd, Plymbridge House, Estover Road, Plymouth PL6 7PY, United Kingdom.
Tel: +44 (0) 1752 202368 Fax: +44 (0) 1752 202330.

British Library Cataloguing-in-Publication Data
A catalogue record for this book is available from the British Library

ISBN 0 7463 0809 4

Typeset by PDQ Typesetting, Newcastle-under-Lyme
Printed and bound in the United Kingdom

for Bryan Loughrey

who cajoled me into writing this

Contents

Preface

At the time of my writing this study Brian Patten is 50 years old, and almost thirty years have passed since the publication in 1967 of his first poetry collection, *Little Johnny's Confession*, and the inclusion of a selection of his work, along with work by Adrian Henri and Roger McGough, in *Penguin Modern Poets No. 10: The Mersey Sound*. Patten was 21 years old when these collections first appeared. Much of the poetry included in them had been written by the time he was 19.

The Mersey Sound went on to sell some 400,000 copies, and all three of 'The Liverpool Poets' have continued to write and perform successfully – both together and apart – over the intervening decades. They can be credited with having been at the very forefront of the movement to bring poetry to wider audiences, and have in turn influenced a whole new generation of 'performance poets'. In chapter 1 of this study, I review the events that led up to this extraordinary phenomenon.

My main aim, however, is to seek to evaluate Patten's achievement as a distinctive poet in his own right, rather than solely as a so-called 'Liverpool Poet' linked inextricably to his fellow-contributors to *The Mersey Sound* and also by extension to the sixties. In chapter 2 I suggest that Patten's work has always been markedly different from that of his peers, and in the succeeding chapters I aim to trace the poetic development that has occurred since his earliest work was published.

In chapter 2 I also suggest that Patten's work – while always popular with the public – has often been undervalued in the past by literary critics. My contention in this study is that the recent publication of *Armada*, his first adult poetry collection for eight years, marks a crucial stage in his maturity as a poet. I believe that the time is now right for a major re-evaluation of his achievement, and I hope that in its small way this study may begin to pave the way for this.

My primary focus is on Patten's career as a serious writer for adults. He is also, however, equally well known as a best-selling writer for children. I have therefore included an Afterword to the study, which offers a necessarily brief overview of this area of Patten's work and achievement.

Acknowledgements

The author and the publishers are grateful to Brian Patten, HarperCollins Publishers and Puffin Books Ltd for permission to quote from the published works of Brian Patten, for adults and children respectively.

Thanks are also due to Brian Patten for generously making private papers available to the author in preparation of this manuscript. Any otherwise unattributed comments by Brian Patten cited in the following study occurred in conversations with the author.

Thanks are due in addition to Adrian Henri and Roger McGough, who have kindly assisted with the factual accuracy of chapters 1 and 2.

Biographical Outline

1946 7 February: Brian Patten born in Liverpool. He is brought up by his grandparents and his mother, Stella, in Wavertree Vale, until his mother's marriage to David Bevan in 1962.

1961 Patten leaves Sefton Park Secondary Modern School and takes a job as a cub reporter on the *Bootle Times*.
November: Patten meets Roger McGough and Adrian Henri, and begins to perform poetry at Liverpool venues.

1962 Patten starts *Underdog*, a poetry magazine in which most of his, McGough's and Henri's early work is first published. It runs for eight issues until 1966.

1963 Patten moves to Canning Street in Liverpool 8, and leaves his job at the *Bootle Times*. Over the next three years he is Liverpool-based, but spends some time abroad in Paris, Dublin, Spain and Tangier.

1967 Patten leaves Liverpool and moves to Winchester.
Spring: publication of Patten's first poetry collection, *Little Johnny's Confession* (Allen and Unwin).
Summer: Patten's work is included in *Penguin Modern Poets No. 10: The Mersey Sound*, along with the work of Henri and McGough.

1969 Publication of *Notes to the Hurrying Man* (Allen and Unwin).
Patten moves to London, where he still remains. He makes a living as a full-time writer, supporting his income with readings.

1970 Patten begins a five-year relationship with Mary Moore, daughter of the sculptor Henry Moore.
Publication of *The Elephant and the Flower*, Patten's first book for children (Allen and Unwin).

1971   Publication of *The Irrelevant Song* (Allen and Unwin).

1972   Publication of children's book *Jumping Mouse* (Allen and Unwin).

1975   Publication of children's book *Mr Moon's Last Case* (Allen and Unwin).
First performance of *The Pig and the Junkle* (play for children).

1976   Publication of *Vanishing Trick* (Allen and Unwin).
Publication of children's book *Emma's Doll* (Allen and Unwin).

1977   Publication of children's book *The Sly Cormorant and the Fishes* (Viking Kestrel).

1979   Publication of *Grave Gossip* (Allen and Unwin).

1980   First performance of *The Ghosts of Riddle-me-Heights* (play for children).

1981   Publication of poetry selection *Love Poems*, drawn from previous collections (Allen and Unwin).
Editor of *Clare's Countryside: Natural History Poetry and Prose by John Clare* (Heinemann/Quixote Press).

1982   First performance of *The Mouthtrap* (play co-written and performed with Roger McGough).

1983   BBC Radio 4 broadcast of *Blind Love* (play).
Publication of *New Volume*, a selection of recent poems by Patten, McGough and Henri (Penguin).

1985   Publication of children's poetry book *Gargling with Jelly* (Puffin Books).

1988   Publication of children's book *Jimmy Tag-Along* (Puffin Books).
Publication of *Storm Damage* (Unwin Hyman).
First performance of *Gargling with Jelly – The Play!* (play for children); playscript published 1991 (Samuel French).

1990   Publication of children's poetry book *Thawing Frozen Frogs* (Puffin Books).
Publication of *Grinning Jack: Selected Poems*, drawn from previous collections (Unwin Hyman).

1991   Editor of *The Puffin Book of Twentieth-Century Children's Verse*.

1992   Publication of children's book *Grizzelda Frizzle and Other Stories* (Puffin Books).

1993   Publication of children's poetry book *The Magic Bicycle* (Walker Books).

1994   13 March: death of Irene Stella Bevan, Patten's mother. Publication of children's book *Impossible Parents* (Walker Books). Publication of children's poetry book *The Utter Nutters* (Puffin Books).

1995   National tour as a performer in *Words on the Run*, with Roger McGough, Adrian Henri, musician Andy Roberts and playwright Willy Russell.

1996   Publication of *Armada* (HarperCollins).

A Note on the Texts

Patten's first five poetry collections – *Little Johnny's Confession*, *Notes to the Hurrying Man*, *The Irrelevant Song*, *Vanishing Trick* and *Grave Gossip* – are no longer in print as discrete volumes. However, the majority of poems from these collections have been reprinted within the two substantial selections *Love Poems* (1981) and *Grinning Jack* (1990) that have been formed from his early work.

When quoting from Patten's first five collections in this study, therefore, I give both the source volume reference and a reference to the selection in which the poem can now be found. Where no second reference is given, this is because the poem cited is not included in either of the subsequent selections. As Patten made a small number of changes to existing poems when assembling *Love Poems* and *Grinning Jack*, I have further adopted the policy of quoting from the versions of the poems printed in the later selections, since these offer the most up-to-date authorial editing.

All of Patten's poetry for adults until *Armada* – his most recent collection – was initially published by Allen and Unwin or (latterly) Unwin Hyman. Now that Unwin Hyman has become a part of HarperCollins Publishers, both *Armada* and his other volumes for adults – namely, *Love Poems*, *Grinning Jack* and *Storm Damage* – are published by HarperCollins under their Flamingo imprint.

Allen and Unwin were also the initial publishers of Patten's earlier works for children – *The Elephant and the Flower*, *Jumping Mouse*, *Mr Moon's Last Case* and *Emma's Doll*. Although the former is at present out of print, *Jumping Mouse* is included within *Grizzelda Frizzle and Other Stories* published by Puffin Books. *Mr Moon's Last Case* is published by Puffin Books, and *Emma's Doll* is currently being republished – also by Puffin Books. Other publishers of Patten's children's work are as listed in the Biographical Outline (pages xii-xiv).

1

The Early Years:
1946–1967

CHILDHOOD

Brian Patten was born in Liverpool on 7 February 1946. His mother, Stella, was 18 years old, and had separated from his father shortly after he was born.

His childhood was working-class. Apart from a brief period in a children's home in Wales, he lived with his mother and grandparents in a cramped terraced house in Wavertree Vale, the street described in 'Lament for the Angels Who've Left My Street' in *Little Johnny's Confession*:

> Streets everywhere! All peopled by memories and the times
> I was a monster and scared my playmates
> On backyard walls cutting clotheslines
> Keeping impossible monkeys in impossible jamjars,
> Playing games in the kickthecan streets and swinging
> On lamps that were then gas and black.

The area was deprived and dilapidated. 'As a child,' he recalled in 1975, in an article in the *Liverpool Daily Post*, 'my playground was the railway embankments; the back-alleys; the bombsites and the derelict houses.'

The atmosphere in the family home was tense and claustrophobic. Three generations were crammed, bickering, into uncomfortable proximity. Patten's grandmother, who had previously been a dancer in music hall, had been crippled in a wartime bombing raid, and her shattered legs were encased in the callipers that become in 'Echoes' (*Armada*) a symbol of the environment's corrosive confinement, both spiritual and physical:

The frightening heartbeat of the house
Is made by her iron callipers.
The bomb-crushed legs, the bolted bones,
The hands that scrape like talons on the stairs,
The damned-up pain, the hate, the grief;
The soul crushed by iron callipers.

What he later described as 'the crushed hopes' and 'stifled longings' within the household weighed heavily on Patten's childhood self. Still – in his own words – 'inarticulate to express the pain felt by the adults around me', he nevertheless began to develop in his isolation the observational stance and capacity for intense introspection that have since come to characterize much of his poetry. 'The Eavesdropper' in *Armada* is rooted in a childhood memory of separateness:

I sat like a cabin-boy who listens in secret
to the crew of a great, creaking ship,
and eavesdropped on the adults below me.

One further adult was part of the household, for a number of years: Lizzy Graham, the 'old woman with a well-worn soul' whose kindness to Patten is recalled in 'Cheque for a Dream' in *Little Johnny's Confession*. Although no relation to the family, she lived with them (sleeping on a chair in the kitchen) and was fond of the solitary child in their midst. Sometimes she would take him to evening shows at the Magnet cinema. (The Magnet was just that for the young Patten – drawing him every Saturday into the alternative universes of 'celluloid imaginations' described in 'Where Are You Now Superman?', in *Little Johnny's Confession*.) In the elegiac 'Cheque for a Dream', also in *Little Johnny's Confession*, her importance in his life is recognized in a touching valedictory image:

Growing's a strange thing Lizzy,
And I have learnt to forget so much.
I don't think of you very often
But when I do I imagine in a cinema a movie screen
Depicting the tenements and old prams and scenery I know so well,

And through it all your sad figure creeps
With Chaplin movements, and sometimes you turn around
And smiling wave at the empty auditorium. But only memories
Clap back and cheer you from the dusty seats.

2

The other female influence in Patten's childhood was Frieda, a refugee from Central Europe who rented a council house further down the road and was regarded by the neighbours as distinctly odd, largely because of her strange habits of dress and her fondness for literature and culture. Wavertree Vale was not generally a place for enquiry, as 'Lament for the Angels Who've Left My Street' (*Little Johnny's Confession*) flatly observes:

> In my street people were mostly happy because they didn't know too much about the state of things,
> They didn't want to know too much about the state of things.

Coming from a near-bookless household (the one and only book owned by the family was a book about foxes), Patten was fascinated by Frieda's eccentricity, but above all by her library. She is described with great affection in his introduction to his anthology *The Puffin Book of Twentieth-Century Children's Verse* (1991), and – interviewed in 1994 in *The Times Educational Supplement* – he recalled:

> She lived about seven doors down from me in a rather dark little house with lots and lots of books. It always smelt of real coffee, which seemed very exotic then ... So I'd go there and she'd lend me books and play opera with very scratchy records. And her house was like a different world. I don't know how she got washed up on our street.

By then, Patten was 10 years old. His passion for reading had been slow-starting, not least because of a difficulty with spelling that still lingers. (In 1981, to his amusement, a CSE English examination question asked pupils to comment on a spelling mistake retained by accident in an early published version of 'Little Johnny's Final Letter', on the mistaken assumption that the error was intentional.) 'Aphasia', in *Storm Damage*, which begins 'I'm seven, and I'm dead bright, | But words give me a fright', gives an insight into his empathy with people struggling to make language work for them:

> Words are mean. They bully me.
> Lock me away
> From what I want to say

At Sefton Park Secondary Modern School he was firmly consigned to the 'C' stream, as bored and rebellious a pupil as the disaffected class in 'Little Johnny's Change of Personality':

> Please Mr Teacher, Sir,
> Turn round from your blackboard,
> Your chalks are crumbling
> Your cane's decaying,
> Turn round from your blackboard
> We're thinking of leaving.
>
> (*Little Johnny's Confession / Grinning Jack*)

Patten's deep scorn for the uninspired schooling he received in these years and consequent mistrust of 'academics' can be traced throughout his poetry. At classroom level, it ranges from the reference in 'Schoolboy' (*Little Johnny's Confession / Grinning Jack*) to the 'Poet dying of| Too much education' to the complacent rant of the cynical schoolteacher in *Storm Damage*'s 'Dead Thick' ('No. I haven't kept up with the modern stuff.| Haven't read a book in years.') Most recently – and most successfully – it resurfaces in 'The Minister for Exams' in *Armada*, although contempt for individual failed teachers has now shifted to informed anger against the impossible bureaucracies of assessment that can stifle children's learning.

In 1960, however – at the start of Patten's final year at school – his experience of education and, indeed, his life began dramatically to alter. The headmaster at Sefton Park School, a Mr Woolley, happened by chance to read an essay that he had written, was swift to recognize an imaginative talent and spirited him hastily into the 'A' stream. There, for the first time, he was given the encouragement to write poetry. 'Writing poetry became an obsession in my last year at school, when I was fourteen', Patten wrote in 1975, in a Puffin Books children's magazine. 'During the times I was unhappy I wrote about my feelings and it helped me understand them better... I was obviously not always unhappy, but seeing lots of unhappiness about me I began to write about that.'

At 14, Patten began to attend evening creative writing classes at the Liverpool Institute. He was also reading voraciously. Among the first books of poetry he read was a volume of works by poets of the First World War. 'Sleep Now', dedicated to the war poet Wilfred Owen (1893–1918), was written when Patten was still only 15 years old, and is an astonishingly mature

4

achievement. Taking its title from the last line of Owen's 'Strange Meeting', it shows already an assured assimilation of many of the dominant moods and images of Owen's own poetry, as well as a glimpse of the individual lyrical voice that Patten was beginning to develop:

> Sleep now,
> Your blood moving in the quiet wind;
> No longer afraid of the rabbits
> Hurrying through the tall grass
> Or the faces laughing from
> The beach and among cold trees.
>
> .   .   .   .
>
> Sleep now,
> Your words have passed
> The lights shining from the East
> And the sound of flak
> Raping graves and emptying seasons.
>
> *(Little Johnny's Confession / Grinning Jack)*

Before long, he was also reading Walt Whitman, and – encouraged by a friend studying French at the university – translations of Rimbaud (in particular) as well as of Baudelaire, Verlaine and Apollinaire. Partly it was Rimbaud's youth that first drew Patten to his work. His poetry had first been published when he was a teenager. But Patten was also attracted by the immediacy of the language of these poets, and what he saw as their direct relevance to ordinary experience. In Apollinaire, for example, he found a poet who could write evocatively of urban life:

> You are walking in Paris now all alone in a crowd
> Herds of mooing buses pass by as you go.
>
> (Apollinaire, 'Zone', trans. Dudley Fitts)

In an interview in the *Guardian* in 1971 he explained this particular appeal:

> That was the poetry which really stimulated me to take an interest. You get out of school at 15 and go straight into this world of police sirens and people rushing about and mucking each other up. The poetry I first liked related to this life.

By 1961, Patten was impatient to leave school. Home life had also acquired new complications, following his mother's marriage to David Bevan, a local policeman, and her move to his house in Underley Street. Patten chose to remain with his grandparents in the year following the marriage. The family atmosphere was even less harmonious at Underley Street than it had been at Wavertree Vale. Bevan was an alcoholic, given to violent and drunken rages in which he would assault both his wife and his stepson. In the disquieting poem 'Little Johnny's Night Visitor', which was added to later editions of *Little Johnny's Confession* and appears in *Grinning Jack*, the child-persona cringes from the sinister 'bogey-man' advancing into his bedroom:

> Last night,
>   before sleep could rescue me
>   the bogey-man came.
>   Drunk, he stumbled over words
>   he will never repeat again.
>
> Father,
>   please do not stare at me.
>   Do not come so close.
>   I do not know how to love strangers.

Spurred on by a visiting Careers Officer's insistence that without formal qualifications he should give up any hopes of a writing career, Patten responded with a determination that would become characteristic and submitted a battery of applications for newspaper jobs. He was taken on by the *Bootle Times* as a cub reporter in April 1961. He worked on the paper for two years (describing it in the *Guardian* in 1969 as 'a surrealist tea-party of a place, where I covered seedy little court cases and vicars' garden fêtes in the one day') before abandoning it for a series of odd jobs (including selling newspapers on the pier) until he could support himself full-time by writing and performing. It was over that two-year period with the *Bootle Times* that his remarkable transformation into a 15-year-old literary entrepreneur began to take shape.

'THE LIVERPOOL SCENE'

Patten continued to live with his family until he was 17, joining his mother and stepfather at Underley Street in early 1963. In the summer of that year, however, his mother attempted suicide following a further drunken assault by his stepfather. Patten took her to hospital. When she recovered, he moved out for good and headed for a rented attic in 32 Canning Street, the subject of the poems 'Room' and 'After Breakfast' in *Little Johnny's Confession / Grinning Jack* and the likely inspiration for Little Johnny's chosen hideaway in 'Little Johnny's Final Letter' in the same collections:

> I've rented a room without any curtains
> and sit behind the windows growing cold.

At various points over the next few years he was to leave the city for short periods to travel to locations that included Paris (where he stayed for a time with the French poet Guy Jequesson at the offices of the Communist paper *L'Humanité* and spent a brief spell earning money by chalking poems on pavements), Dublin (staying with the playwright John Arden), Spain and Tangier. For the rest of his time in Liverpool, however, Canning Street remained Patten's base.

By the time Patten chose to move there, Canning Street – the main artery of Liverpool's scruffily cosmopolitan District 8 – was already very well known to him. George Melly memorably described the character of 'Liverpool 8' in the *Observer* in 1967:

> Liverpool 8 is a once-fashionable Georgian district now scrawled over with graffiti, scarred with unhealed bomb sites, dominated by the stranded neo-Gothic whale of the Anglican cathedral: a multi-racial slum waiting in raddled beauty for the planners' bulldozers.

It is also evoked in Adrian Henri's prose-poem 'Liverpool 8':

> ...Doric columns supporting peeling entablatures,
> dirty windows out of Vitruvius concealing families of happy
> Jamaicans, sullen out-of-work Irishmen, poets, queers, thieves,
> painters, university students, lovers...

From the early sixties, as Edward Lucie-Smith describes in his introduction to *The Liverpool Scene* (Donald Carroll, 1967), artists, writers and musicians had started to congregate there. On the edge of Liverpool 8, Streate's Coffee Bar in particular became established as their general meeting place. At the same time Streate's had also become a focal point for several London poets, notably Pete Brown and Spike Hawkins, who – along with the scriptwriter Johnny Byrne – introduced their own readings of new poetry in the basement club. A lively sub-culture was beginning to flourish – in defiance both of the existing domination of British popular music by the American influence, and also of the 'inhibitions' and 'pretensions' (in Lucie-Smith's words, p. 6) of the distant London literary establishment.

In the poetry that Lucie-Smith was later to include in *The Liverpool Scene*, the working-class character of the city was upheld as a source of pride, and the characteristic throwaway wit of its inhabitants was celebrated in verse that was typically humorous, colloquial and rooted in urban realities. Above all, in keeping with the oral traditions perpetuated by the strong Irish influence within the city, Livepool's new wave of poets worked with the spoken rather than the written word. 'The poetry now being written in Liverpool', wrote Lucie-Smith, 'differs from other contemporary English verse because it has made its impact by being spoken and listened to, rather than read' (p. 3).

In October 1961, attracted by an advertisement in the *Liverpool Echo* that said 'Meet Pete the Beat at Streate's', Patten made his first visit to Streate's Coffee Bar and quickly became first a part and then a leading light of its circles. On 2 November 1961, he was given a brief slot to read two poems – his first public performance. He was fifteen years old. Then on 6 November, at Streate's again, he met Roger McGough for the first time. Three days later they performed together at a reading at Hope Hall (now the Everyman Theatre), where he met Adrian Henri whom McGough had already known for some while. The group of three writers who would come – partly by an accident of publishing – to be known as the Liverpool Poets had now formed, although none could be aware of that at the time. All continued to write and perform – either separately or together – within the wider circuit that still included Brown and Hawkins, and across a range of Liverpool pub and club venues that mushroomed as the bohemian reputation of Liverpool 8's sub-culture gathered currency.

All three poets recall the energy and comparative innocence of these early days with some affection. Interviewed in the *Guardian* in 1983, Henri explained:

What was interesting about those early years was that the Liverpool audience accepted us as a kind of alternative entertainment, not culture... It was just a night out for them.

In 1989, in an interview with *Monitor*, an Auckland University student newspaper, Patten also spoke of the ready eclecticism that had prevailed among audiences:

There was a lot of energy around and we'd go to various clubs where you'd get comedians, playwrights, sportsmen and villains all in one place simply because it was a small city. Somebody might say 'What do you do?' and the reply would be 'I'm a footballer' or 'I'm a poet' or 'I'm a villain' and there would be acceptance totally, as long as you were straight with it.

McGough, quoted in *The Liverpool Scene*, remembered, above all, the audiences' openness to experience:

At the readings we did every Monday night at Samson and Barlow's the kids didn't look on it as Poetry with a capital 'P', they looked on it as modern entertainment, part of the pop movement. They may go away crying, or they may go away very sad, but it was a certain experience for them, all part of experience. (p. 79)

The work of the three Liverpool Poets as a group is looked at in more detail in chapter 2. However, it is worth underlining immediately that they were then – and are still – in many ways very different. Patten was significantly younger (McGough was born in 1937, and Henri in 1932). Nor did he share their university backgrounds: McGough had studied French and Geography at Hull, and Henri had studied Fine Art at Durham. Both McGough and Henri were teaching at the time when the threesome came together, the former at a comprehensive school and the latter at Liverpool College of Art. And, interestingly, Henri was at that point first and foremost a painter, having last written poetry in the fifties. Nevertheless, they were to write and perform together increasingly over the next few years, and – most importantly – Patten was to sow the seeds for the success that was later to follow by publishing both their work and his own in his magazine *Underdog*.

Patten started *Underdog* in 1962. He was just turning 16 years old, and was now organizing as well as performing at readings in an ever-expanding range of venues as the 'Liverpool scene' gained momentum. *Underdog* was the first magazine to publish many of the then underground poets and is widely acknowledged not only to have broken new ground but also to have had a lasting influence on the many similar enterprises that would follow. The poet Michael Horovitz, in his anthology of 'Underground' poetry, *Children of Albion* (Penguin, 1969), is unequivocal in his view of Patten's significance:

> Brian Patten is the man most responsible for building the *actual* Liverpool scene with his plangent erotic saxophonetrance voice, & a scrutable sincerity – evoked also in his littlest, purest of little mags – *Underdog*. (p. 328)

The first issue of *Underdog* appears not to have survived. The second includes work by McGough, Patten and a number of local poets (plus a number of column-filling poems by Patten operating under a variety of *noms de plume*). By issues three and four, at which point Patten had joined forces with Eddie O'Neill who became co-editor and took responsibility for printing the magazine, *Underdog* had developed from its initial ten-page Roneo stencil format into a professional booklet, and its range of contributors had extended. By the time of the last two issues (seven and eight) in 1965 and 1966, it was publishing writers of international stature – including the American poets Allen Ginsberg and Robert Creeley, the Finnish poet Pentii Saarikoski and the Russian poet Andrei Voznesensky (in translations by Anselm Hollo), and (in translation by Adrian Henri) the French poet Jacques Prévert. In the final issue Patten included 'Little Johnny's Confession' and 'The Beast', arguably the two most significant of his own earliest poems (see chapter 3).

By then the 'Liverpool scene' was at its zenith. The musical innovation that had been taking place alongside art and literary experiments had exploded triumphantly onto the national and international music market with the unprecedented success of the Beatles, and a number of similar bands. The city became world-famous. The American poet Allen Ginsberg raved enthusiastically in *The Liverpool Scene* that 'Liverpool is at the present moment the centre of the consciousness of the human universe' (p. 15). The writings of Liverpool's poet-performers began suddenly to attract serious attention from the London-based media. A huge poetry spectacular at London's Royal Albert Hall in June 1965, in which Patten participated, attracted

10

a massive audience of almost 5,000, and set the stage for two similar events at the Royal Festival Hall, in which he would also take part: the Poetry Gala in February 1969 (where participants included Basil Bunting, Ted Hughes and Stevie Smith), and the Festival of Poetry with Music in May 1972 (which included readings by Pablo Neruda and Stephen Spender). 'Performance poetry', as it came to be known much later, was suddenly fashionable.

In 1965 the energies of Patten and his contemporaries were rewarded. The BBC sent a radio crew up to Liverpool to record Patten reading 'Little Johnny's Confession' for Jack de Manio's breakfast radio show. When it was broadcast, Philip Unwin, of the publishers, Allen and Unwin, happened to be listening whilst shaving, and was impressed. He discovered the address of the poet's digs, rang his landlady, and – on her landing – Patten took the call offering him his first book deal. At 19 he was suddenly on his way to becoming a professional poet.

Meanwhile, McGough was also attracting a book contract with Michael Joseph for *Frinck, a Life in the Day of and Summer with Monika* (Henri's *Tonight at Noon* (Rapp & Whiting) would follow in 1968), and Penguin was selecting the poets to include in its forthcoming *Modern Poets* anthology. The title – picking up on the pun on the Sound of the River Mersey, which had given Liverpool's music scene its name – was to be *The Mersey Sound*.

THE LEAVING OF LIVERPOOL

In spring 1967, *Little Johnny's Confession* was published by Allen and Unwin. In summer 1967, Patten's work appeared – with that of McGough and Henri – in *Penguin Modern Poets No. 10: The Mersey Sound*, a paperback imprint retailing at three shillings and sixpence (17.5p) and destined to become one of the best-selling poetry collections of this century. Patten was the youngest poet to be represented in the series.

Ironically, before publication of either, Patten had fled the city – alarmed by the publicity machine gathering momentum around him, as he recalled ruefully in an interview with the *Observer* in 1983:

> The media descended on Liverpool trying to get us to do records

11

and become part of the pop thing... I wanted nothing to do with publicity... I just wanted to write poetry.

He has never returned to Liverpool to live. After a year or so living in Winchester, he settled in London and has been based there ever since (although with intermittent periods in Italy, Majorca, Devon and Cornwall). In an article written for the *Liverpool Daily Post* in 1975, however, he acknowledged the lasting influence that the city had had – and would continue to have – on him:

> Nobody born in the city – and I mean the city, not its outskirts, bleak and new and soulless – can ever really leave. The city is within them... Its images and memories are so powerful they will remain with me forever; Liverpool I carry within me, from the first breath to the last.

Patten's words were prophetic. One aim of this study will be to consider the lasting influence of his Liverpool upbringing on his poetry, culminating in his triumphant spiritual return to confront the ghosts of his childhood in *Armada*.

2

'Poets of the Sixties'

THE LIVERPOOL POETS

Even though there were still quite a number of other poets writing and performing in Liverpool, publication of the Penguin anthology in 1967 meant that Patten, McGough and Henri inevitably became *the* Liverpool Poets from then on.

The label has perhaps brought rather more disadvantages than advantages over the years. The city has become – through the Beatles – almost inextricably linked in the national (and even international) consciousness with the 1960s, a decade which itself comes complete with a standard set of related – and very superficial – images of flower power, drug culture, 'free love' and so on. As an initial label of place, therefore, 'Liverpool' has had the effect by association of also anchoring the poets both to a particular time and to an assumed set of values. Interestingly, apart from the odd reference to 'getting stoned on milk' ('Schoolboy' in *Little Johnny's Confession / Grinning Jack*) and the occasional unwise foray into psychedelic musings (such as 'Old Crock' in *Notes to the Hurrying Man / Grinning Jack*), the poetry Patten wrote in the 1960s is considerably less locked into that culture than is generally assumed. 'Little Johnny Takes a Trip to Another Planet', for example, in *Little Johnny's Confession / Grinning Jack*, is almost universally taken to refer to an LSD hallucination – a reading that the poet insists is incorrect:

> I was always suspicious, being a working class Liverpool lad, of the gurus around in the sixties. 'The Prophet's Good Idea' [in *Notes to the Hurrying Man / Grinning Jack*] was a satire on them. The flower power culture was one I didn't really feel at home in. I never took to wearing beads or bells. I felt alien to that culture, although it embraced my work.

Similarly, the poem 'Through the Tall Grass In Your Head' in *Notes to the Hurrying Man / Grinning Jack* has a hippie-sounding title, but is in fact a poem about Patten's grandfather.

If it is potentially misleading to approach even the poetry Patten originally wrote in the 1960s with too many preconceptions based on general assumptions about the era, it is clearly even less productive to approach his later poetry from this perspective. In that respect, therefore, the 'Liverpool' tag has become something of a millstone.

The other problem with the 'Liverpool Poets' grouping is that the term does not allow for differentiation. It implies that the work of the three poets are essentially interchangeable – or, at the very least, that the early works (which were written at the time when the term first originated and gained currency) might be so. In fact, this is not true at all – indeed, rather the opposite is the case. Reviewing the three separate collections assembled in the expanded edition of *The Mersey Sound* (1974), it is surprisingly difficult to identify significant similarities between Patten's work as represented in that collection and the work of Henri and McGough, beyond a shared urban territory and – crucially – a common preoccupation with directness of expression.

Similarities between the early works of Henri and McGough are more apparent. Both, for example, are conscious humorists – especially relishing the anarchic possibilities of word-play. Henri's 'Song for a Beautiful Girl Petrol-Pump Attendant on the Motorway' is a simple example:

> I wanted your soft verges
> But you gave me the hard shoulder

Here, the play on words (on 'cold shoulder' meaning sexual brush-off) is used for purely comic effect. In other poems, the introduction of an unexpected juxtaposition can provoke a more complex reaction. In 'Let Me Die a Youngman's Death', for example, McGough superimposes matter (a cancerous growth) on to mood (the pun on 'humour') to achieve an effect that is much more disquieting:

> When I'm 73
> & in constant good tumour

Henri – who, of the three poets, has the most explicitly theoretical approach – describes this verbal ingenuity in *Tonight At Noon* as 'the re-evaluation of the cliché':

This seems to be one of the most interesting aspects of what the Liverpool poets and some other English poets are doing. The cliché is a living piece of language that has gone dead through overwork. At any time it can be energised or revitalized. Often by changing its context, putting it in an alien context, contradicting its apparent meaning... (p. 80)

Thus, in Henri's 'Batpoem' the familiar 'Batman' theme tune of the sixties with its three repeated wails of 'Batman!' is reworked into a blatantly non-heroic anthem. The speaker's interest in the clichéd 'damsels in distress' is as would-be seducer rather than as gallant rescuer, and a version of the contraceptive pill has been appropriated as an additional weapon in the infamous arsenal of Bat-gadgets:

> Take me back to Gotham City
> Batman
> Take me where the girls are pretty
> Batman
>
> All those damsels in distress
> Half-undressed or even less
> The Batpill makes 'em all say Yes
> Batman

McGough also has fun with his superheroes. In 'Goodbat Nightman' the 'Bat' metaphor becomes literal, with the Caped Crusader and his Boy Wonder sidekick transformed into real (vampire) bats in a verse form that parodies A. A. Milne's well-known bedtime poem:

> They've had a hard day
> helping clean up the town.
> Now they hang from the mantelpiece
> both upside down.
>
> A glass of warm blood
> and then straight up the stairs,
> Batman and Robin
> are saying their prayers.

(Notably, the 'Batman' poem by Patten in *The Mersey Sound* could

15

hardly be more different from Henri's or McGough's zany contributions. 'Where Are You Now, Batman?' – a reworking of 'Where Are You Now, Superman?' from *Little Johnny's Confession* and published also in *Grinning Jack* – is a lament for the loss of his childhood 'celluloid companions' to 'That Ghastly Adversary, | Mr Old Age'. It ends ominously as the enemy approaches, 'His machine-gun dripping with years'.)

A further similarity between Henri and McGough at the time of *The Mersey Sound* was their active involvement in pop music, and – unlike Patten – both of them frequently incorporated music into poetry performances. Henri led a poetry/rock group known as 'Liverpool Scene' from 1967 until 1970. More famously, McGough was a member of 'The Scaffold', with John Gorman and Mike McGear (the brother of Paul McCartney). The group had three *Top Ten* hit records, including a Number One with 'Lily the Pink'.

Musical influence – primarily drawn from blues music – is particularly prominent in Henri's work. The poem 'The Midnight Hour' is titled after a Wilson Pickett Song; the poem and collection *Tonight at Noon* take their joint title from an LP by Charlie Mingus; and a number of poems (such as 'Who?') draw their detail from Henri's record collection:

> Who can I
> listen to Georges Brassens
> singing
> '*Les amoureux des bancs publiques*'
> with
>
> . . . .
> Who
> can I
> buy
> my next Miles Davis record
> to share with

Other poems explicitly take on the rhythms and conventions of blues songs, often for the purposes of parody. 'Adrian Henri's Talking After Christmas Blues' begins:

> Well I woke up this mornin' it was Christmas Day

'Car Crash Blues or Old Adrian Henri's Interminable Talking Surrealistic Blues' – dedicated to the unlikely combination of the

American painter Jim Dine and the French poet Baudelaire – takes no chances with the prospect of being taken seriously:

> You make me feel like
> someone's driven me into a wall
> baby
> You make me feel like
> Sunday night at the village hall
> baby
> You make me feel like a Desert Rat
> You make me feel like a Postman's hat
> You make me feel like I've been swept under the mat
> baby.

A further influence on Henri – not shared with either McGough or Patten – is his background as a painter, which had a particular impact on the form of his early poetry. Frequently, for example, he juxtaposes visual images with advertising slogans, newspaper headlines or lists of names to create a montage effect that parallels some of the mixed-media techniques used in 1960s Pop Art. 'The New, Fast, Automatic Daffodils', for example, is described in *The Mersey Sound* as a 'cut-up of Wordsworth's poem plus a Dutch motor car leaflet'. Probably the most extreme example of his assimilation at that time of methods and approaches imported from Fine Art is the poem 'Me' which is prefaced by the question *'if you weren't you who would you like to be?'* The poem comprises a list of over eighty names, beginning:

> Paul McCartney Gustav Mahler
> Alfred Jarry John Coltrane
> Charlie Mingus Claude Debussy
> Wordsworth Monet Bach and Blake

and continuing in this vein for a further eleven stanzas. It is up to the reader to respond impressionistically and to navigate a route through the associations.

McGough's early experiments with form, by contrast, were more obviously literary. Like the American poet e. e. cummings, for example, he adopts a consciously flexible approach in some poems to typography – for instance, by using the lower case letter 'i', or by varying layout to convey an additional visual dimension of meaning as in 'There's Something Sad', where the

17

poem itself visibly shrinks away from its subject:

> Like the girl with the hair-lip
> whom
> no one
> wants
> to
> kiss.

McGough's poems in *The Mersey Sound* also show extensive experiment with word-blends and compound adjectives, very much in the manner of both e. e. cummings and Dylan Thomas. In 'The Icingbus' the influence of cummings is almost too apparent. The ghost of cummings's 'little| lame balloonman' does not seem quite far enough away:

> the littleman
> with the hunchbackedback
> creptto his feet
> to offer his seat
> to the blindlady

Conversely, the excellent first and final stanzas of 'Let Me Die a Youngman's Death' have a richness and vitality of language that recall Thomas at his best, without in any way compromising the originality of McGough's poem:

> Let me die a youngman's death
> not a clean & inbetween
> the sheets holywater death
> not a famous-last-words
> peaceful out of breath death
> . . . .
> Let me die a youngman's death
> not a free from sin tiptoe in
> candle wax & waning death
> not a curtains drawn by angels borne
> 'what a nice way to go' death

Here McGough is at his most powerful, demonstrating not only a confident control of verbal register and image (with which he is generally adept) but also a fine technical mastery. The rhythm of the poem becomes akin to incantation, as the impetus of the insistent repetitions within both stanzas (lines two and four begin with 'not'; lines one, three and five end with 'death') is reinforced and given solidity by a forceful pattern of internal rhyme ('clean'/'between'; 'breath'/'death'; 'sin'/'in'; 'drawn'/ 'borne').

'Let Me Die a Youngman's Death' is an example of a poem in which humour and seriousness successfully blend, and this is very much a characteristic of the best of McGough's and Henri's early work. There are still differences between them, as has been emphasized. McGough's world is on the whole a gentler, more domestic city world than Henri's, for example. It has aunts and uncles, bus conductors and bus conductresses, hot dog sellers, fish and chip shops. The tone of McGough's more serious poetry is also usually more wistful, less strident. He has a talent for focusing on evocative detail, such as the twisted wheelchair in 'The Fallen Birdman' or the thighbones emerging from old battlefields in 'On Picnics', and for creating small but touching vignettes, such as the imaginary priest queuing for his supper in 'Vinegar'. While the majority of Henri's more serious poetry in *The Mersey Sound* is intellectual in conception and demands a rational rather than an emotional response, McGough's poetry in the same volume works also through the feelings.

Patten, on the other hand, exerts his appeal almost *entirely* through the feelings, and this – above all else – is what separates him from the others. His poetry is complementary to Henri's and McGough's and may often share issues and concerns – but essentially it is of a different nature, as I hope the succeeding chapters will demonstrate. And while his work may contain elements of humour – although the early poems, in fact, contain comparatively little – that humour is of an entirely different character to the verbal gymnastics of Henri and McGough, and it is subordinated almost always to an underlying seriousness of purpose.

Patten's seriousness also differentiated him as a performer at this early stage. The critic Grevel Lindop drew attention to this in his chapter 'Poetry, Rhetoric and the Mass Audience: The Case of the Liverpool Poets' in *British Poetry Since 1960* (Carcanet Press, 1972), making a comparison in particular between Patten and McGough:

> McGough's style of reading is very attractive: in the old Everyman Theatre in Liverpool, where he seems most at home, he perches on a

high stool, looking like a sad, exotic bird because of both his posture and his flamboyant clothes... His reading – one tends almost to say 'his act' – is meticulously controlled: the moods of the poems are carefully varied, McGough keeping an entirely straight face through even the most comic ones, and one suspects that the audience is constantly being observed for the smallest sign of discontent or boredom. Patten on the other hand seems both more spontaneous and less relaxed. He appears moody, even inarticulate between poems, and the audience is excited, probably, not only by the enormous passion with which he reads (or rather intones or chants) his poems but also by the suspicion that at any moment he may be going to pick a quarrel with someone. (p. 95)

Whatever the rights and wrongs of the latter comment, Lindop is nevertheless highlighting a significant distinctiveness about Patten's reading style in comparison with McGough's or Henri's. Often delivered from memory, with eyes half-closed and hands thrust deep into pockets to hide the tensions, his reading is markedly more sonorous, more concentrated, more intense. In 'The Poet in the Sixties: Vices and Virtues' – a recorded conversation with the poet Peter Porter, transcribed as a chapter in the same book as Lindop's article – Peter Porter characterized Patten as having 'that little touch of moonlight' (p. 207). In fact, Porter's purpose in remarking on this was to mock what he saw as the gullibility of Patten's audience, but he was nevertheless prepared to concede that Patten's reading of his own work was hypnotic. The actor Sir Ian McKellan listed a recording of Patten's reading as one of his favourite spoken voice records (along with recordings by Sir John Gielgud and Dylan Thomas) in an interview in the *Observer* in 1985. The poet Adrian Mitchell, quoted in the jacket copy of the first edition of *Little Johnny's Confession*, has provided perhaps the most enduring description:

> The voice in which he reads his poems has all the colours of a melancholic alto sax, a swaying voice which induces his audience to sweat warm olive oil.

The label of 'Liverpool Poet' has probably ultimately done few favours to any of the three poets of *The Mersey Sound*, but it could be argued that it has been particularly unhelpful to Patten. Without wishing to underestimate the success or the quality of McGough's or Henri's early poetry, I have attempted to suggest that much of it is nevertheless very significantly different in purpose and effect from Patten's. The critic Martin Booth, writing in *British Poetry 1964–84: Driving Through the Barricades* (Routledge & Kegan Paul, 1985), has urged strongly for a separate evaluation of Patten's work:

> From the start, his poetry was different, both from his peers' work and that of anyone else being published. (p. 135)

An aim of this study, as indicated in the Preface, will therefore be to encourage consideration of Patten's poetry apart from – rather than within – the context of the Liverpool Poets as a group.

THE WAR WITH THE 'ESTABLISHMENT'

Speaking in a 1988 BBC 'Radiovision' schools broadcast, Patten identified the key shared concern that he believed linked the Liverpool Poets:

> I think we've influenced each other mainly in the need to make poetry continually accessible to people.

In this aim, all three of the poets have been undeniably – indeed, quite spectacularly – successful. They have proved a notable exception to Adrian Mitchell's ironic 'Rule' that 'Most people ignore most poetry, because most poetry ignores most people', which Patten is fond of quoting. Their success has also, quite clearly, paved the way for new generations of poets to write and perform for audiences that might not in the past have been viewed as typical poetry readers. Just as the Liverpool Poets helped to break down the London/provinces divide and the middle-/working-class divide, so in the 1980s poets such as Linton Kwesi Johnson and Benjamin Zephaniah have attacked the black/white divide and have played their own part in the birth of 'rap' poetry.

With a small number of notable exceptions, however, poetry critics from within the traditional so-called 'Establishment' have shown little enthusiasm for acknowledging that work that is popular may also have literary merit, and reviews of the Liverpool Poets have been at best uneven. Typical approaches have included patronizing dismissals of the poetry's initial audiences as uninformed provincials, as in Stanley Reynolds's well-known put-down (as an American living in Liverpool at the time) in the *Observer* in 1967:

> The fact that the Liverpool people believe that *their* bad poetry is different from other bad poetry ... does not make it so. Seven hundred and forty-five thousand, two hundred and thirty Scousers after all *can* be wrong.

and Peter Porter's further comments in the recorded conversation mentioned on page 20:

> I've found that the only really popular style of poetry... is the pop poetry, the Liverpool cabaret type poetry – you couldn't really dignify it with the name 'cabaret', more the underground shelter sort of poetry. That goes down pretty well. There's a tremendous fondness for anything soft and squashy. (p. 207)

Partly, one senses, critics' discomfort arose from deep suspicion of the performance context that first brought the poets' work to public attention. Anthony Thwaite dismissed performance poets in *Twentieth Century English Poetry* (Heinemann, 1978) as mere crowd-pleasers: 'Henri and the rest are... clowns, entertainers' (p. 124). In the book chapter referred to earlier, Grevel Lindop cited Henri's acknowledgement that poems might change as a result of a reading as evidence that 'the audience thus plays an almost direct part in the organisation of the poetry' (p. 94). He implied that the poems were therefore products of a joint and essentially non-literary collaboration between poet and audience. Quite apart from the oddness of the suggestion that collaboration has no place in creativity, this is clearly an overstatement. Performing to and for an audience, and possibly redrafting as a consequence, is not the same thing as surrendering individual authorship to composition by clapometer. Moreover, Lindop's argument is not aided by his attitude to poetry audiences, which would appear to be marked by the same distaste as Peter Porter's. In a nutshell, Lindop's contention was that the poetry reflected the youth and lack of sophistication of the audiences for whom it was written.

If youth – of both the poets and their audiences – was a problem for some of the contemporary critics, so too was the Liverpool Poets' association – largely through Henri and McGough, as noted earlier – with popular music. To some critics, this alignment between poetry and popular music was seen as a dilution and debasement of an art form. In *Society and Literature 1945–70* (Methuen, 1983), Alan Sinfield instantly sets limits on the poetry's potential by the inverted commas around 'pop'.

> This new 'pop' verse often has a slight lyric grace, some humour, and a pleasing simplicity of diction. There is no doubt, however, that so far its poetic achievement is small, and its notoriety largely a result of public gimmicks. (p. 166)

To the poets, on the other hand, given their commitment to making poetry accessible to wider audiences, the involvement of music was entirely logical. As McGough pointed out in an article in the *Guardian* in 1983, music has already led the way as an art form in reaching broader cross-sections of people:

> It's always seemed to me that if you're writing things and feeling things, if you're sharing it with as many people as possible, all the better. Music seems to work that way. Millions of people go to the Proms but poetry is always seen as belonging to a coterie and you have to be super-sensitive or super-intelligent to understand it. I've never really understood why it should be.

Perhaps because he has tended, however grudgingly, to be singled out as potentially the most 'literary' of the Liverpool Poets, Patten – paradoxically – has sometimes found himself victim of the worst reviews of all. The sense of alienation described in 'The Literary Gathering' in *The Irrelevant Song / Grinning Jack* is unsurprising. Caught in the middle of complicated and vituperative critical rivalries, with critics vying for supremacy and questioning the taste of their peers, his work attracts surprisingly personal attacks. Reviewing *Little Johnny's Confession* in the *Sunday Times* in 1967, Christopher Ricks wondered disingenuously:

> Who poured triple superphosphate fertiliser over Brian Patten's innocence? Too luxuriant, and too luxuriated in, is his childhood wonder at the world.

Over twenty years later, reviewing *Storm Damage* for the *Independent on Sunday* in 1989, Lachlan MacKinnon character-ized the collection in extremely brutal terms as poetry that:

> flickers like the last surviving members of a species of butterfly, a sad memorial to its own failed promise.

23

One obvious source of irritation for 'Establishment' critics has been the receptiveness of a number of eminent 'Establishment' poets to Patten's work. The poet Ted Hughes (now the Poet Laureate) was one of the three-person panel of judges to award him the Eric Gregory prize for a first poetry collection (*Little Johnny's Confession*) in 1967. Charles Causley wrote warmly in his entry on Patten's writing for adults and children in the third edition of *Twentieth Century Children's Writers* (St James Press, 1989):

> He gazes with unwavering curiosity at the minutiae of existence, and at its complexities and clichés. He reveals a sensibility profoundly aware of the ever-present possibility of the miraculous, as well as of the granite-hard realities ... These are all undiluted poems, beautifully calculated, informed – even in their darkest moments – with courage and hope ... Patten, uncompromisingly, goes all out for the poem, not the audience: and the rest follows. (p. 763)

Philip Larkin went one further, and in 1973 included two poems by Patten – 'Portrait of a Young Girl Raped at a Suburban Party' and 'Ode on Celestial Music' – in *The Oxford Book of 20th Century English Verse*, which he edited for Oxford University Press. Both poems were from *Notes to the Hurrying Man*, and are included in *Grinning Jack*. The uproar in rarefied literary circles was immediate. On 29 March 1973, the critic Donald Davie reviewed the anthology in the *Listener*, under the heading 'Larkin's Choice'. The entire focus of his article was to challenge Patten's right to be included (and Larkin's motives in having included him). 'Portrait of a Young Girl Raped at a Suburban Party' was printed in full, with the comment:

> That's it. That's the poem. At no point, by no one of the many ways available has imagination entered, penetrated, opened up, transformed... How Patten got to the point of thinking this sort of thing is a poem is a good and appalling question.

The correspondence was still running on 7 June. Larkin himself wrote in, icily refuting any suggestion that he had not been responsible for the choice of poems. (He also dispatched a supportive postcard to Patten: 'Ignore them. The scissor-men are everywhere.') No correspondent, I note, felt inclined to question the peculiarly sexual nature of Davie's vilification ('entered, penetrated, opened up'), but one correspondent, Ursula Temple, effectively summed up the pro-Patten viewpoint:

> Donald Davie twice defines poetry as 'writing in which language is . . . explored as a medium'. When he has stopped being so excitable over the riff-raff getting in to his Royal Enclosure of Poetry, will he tell us again if he really means this horrible little heresy? Words, words, words, words, words? As a medium of *what*, for God's sake?

Patten maintained a dignified silence during the furore. His response came several years later in *Grave Gossip*, where the poem 'The Critics' Chorus' (subtitled 'Or, What the Poem Lacked') quotes Davie's 'How [he] got to the point of thinking this sort of thing is a poem is a good and appalling question' as its epigraph. The poem, also included in *Grinning Jack*, ironically recalls the critical opprobrium that first greeted the work of a number of talented poets, including Stevie Smith:

> Of course they were right:
> So much of what she wrote was doggerel,
> mere child's play.
>
> *In a London suburb Stevie,*
> *Blake's grandchild,*
> *fingering a rosary made of starlight.*

Each pairing of stanzas sets the dull, dismissive dogmatism of the anonymous 'they' against the brave individuality and imagination of the poets who are scorned. The language of the stanzas entering the world of the poets is rich and sensuous (Rimbaud is pictured *'remembering the jewelled spider webs,* | *The smoking pond'*). And the use of italics reinforces this separateness, as well as giving a visual suggestion of a certain delicacy and fragility. 'The Critics' Chorus' concludes as follows:

> It was something to do with what the poem lacked
> saved it from oblivion,
> a hunger nothing to do with the correct idiom
> in which to express itself
>
> but a need to eat a fruit far off
> from the safe orchard,
> reached by no easy pathway
> or route already mapped.

Patten's argument is clear. The received criteria by which less principled 'Establishment' critics make judgements can come to be their 'safe orchard', their mapped route. Their position is protected. When confronted with work that challenges these criteria and therefore the security and authority of their position, they take refuge in negativity. It is the poet, and not the critic, who has the courage – and the *'need'* – to leave the 'easy pathway'. 'If a poet accepts the challenge of a wider audience', Patten said nearly ten years later, in an interview with the *Sunday Times* in 1988:

> he takes the risk of being ostracised by the academics, partly out of envy, and partly because he takes the work out of their hands.

THIRTY YEARS ON

From the earliest reviews, hostile critics were predicting that the success and popularity of the Liverpool Poets could not survive far beyond the 1960s, because their existing young audience would soon outgrow them and their work would not offer the same appeal to a new generation of young people. Thirty years on, events have proved those critics wrong. Writing in 1972 in the essay noted earlier, Grevel Lindop characterized the Liverpool Poets' audience as 'a young audience':

> it includes few people who one would guess to be over 25, and a mere scattering of the obviously middle-aged.

It was assumed, erroneously, that these under-25-year-olds would cease to follow poetry as and when it was no longer fashionable, and that the work of Liverpool Poets would cease to be of relevance to later audiences of that age group.

More cynically, it was also strongly suggested in some quarters that the poets' talents were in any case too limited to be capable of development and growth. Ian Hamilton, writing in the *Observer* in 1969, was clearly very much of this school of thought when he singled Patten out for the following heavily backhanded compliment:

> Brian Patten is a much-publicised member of the much-publicised Liverpool Scene, and the only one of that rather dismal crew who

has shown even a glimmer of poetic talent. Whether or not his slight gifts will be able to survive the plaudits of fans and the cynical attention of entrepreneurs remains to be seen. But Patten does show tremblings of promise; he is a sensitive, intelligent writer with an excellent ear. One can only hope that he is sensitive and intelligent enough not to be fooled by the current fuss.

Thirty years on, the poets' detractors have been proved wrong on all counts. Book sales and audience figures over the decades have given the lie to the prediction that the poets would lose their public. For example, over the period October 1995 to May 1996 Patten has performed solo to capacity audiences at over twenty venues. Over the same period, the touring show *Words on the Run* – involving Patten, McGough, Henri, the playwright Willy Russell and musician Andy Roberts – has played in major theatres, attracting a total audience of some 6,000 people across the eight performances.

Furthermore, the nature both of the poetry and of the audiences has broadened. Unsurprisingly, some of the early poetry has dated and slipped quietly from the repertoire or been omitted from recent collections. Space travel, for instance, has notably dropped off the agenda. But themes of adolescence, of clashes with authority, of love and loss remain as relevant to today's young audiences as they were in the 1960s. Moreover, today's audiences now also include an older element – many of the original 25-year-olds, now in their 50s, whose staying power Lindop so doubted. Both the poets and their audience have matured and developed. As the poets' own lives have brought changes in experience and outlook, their poetry has evolved accordingly to reflect these changing concerns, and they have succeeded in taking those audiences into age with them.

All three of the Liverpool Poets now write differently and in many ways more interestingly than they did in the days of *The Mersey Sound*, as separate studies of Henri and McGough could also demonstrate. However, it is fair to say that Patten's poetry has led the way in this respect. In his otherwise critical article, Lindop nevertheless acknowledged that the poetry being published by Patten by the time of publication of *British Poetry Since 1960* in 1972 was already shifting significantly in resonance and authority, and noted 'new weight and balance' in his work:

Brian Patten's more recent poetry, as represented by his books *Notes to the Hurrying Man* and *The Irrelevant Song*, seems to be seeking a calm lyricism in which there is, I think an implicit realisation that the hectoring 'public-poet' style of *Little Johnny's Confession* is a *cul-de-sac*, a literary manner that offers no hope of development. (p. 104)

In *British Poetry 1964–84: Driving Through the Barricades*, Martin Booth identified the publication of Patten's next book, *Vanishing Trick*, in 1976 as the moment that 'more or less ended that style of poetry that so typified the school from the Mersey' (p. 114) and affirmed strongly the distinctiveness, influence and integrity of his poetic voice:

Of the Liverpool poets, it was Brian Patten who became the leader and it is he who has maintained his artistic hold and development, leading his ideas and muse on from earlier work to later progressions. If the intention of art is always to be under change and flux then Patten's poetry is just that, for it is not a fixed point but always in motion (p. 136)

In the remainder of this study I shall therefore aim to trace Patten's poetic development, considering his work chronologically from first publication in 1967 to the publication of *Armada* in 1996, assessing the extent to which he has matured as a poet and – as Patten enters his fifties – seeking to establish his entitlement at this stage to serious critical consideration as a significant and successful poet of the twentieth century.

3

Travelling Between Places: Poems 1967–1976

> Leaving nothing and nothing ahead;
> when you stop for the evening
> the sky will be in ruins,
>
> when you hear late birds
> with tired throats singing
> think how good it is that they,
>
> knowing you were coming,
> stayed up late to greet you
> who travels between places
>
> when the late afternoon
> drifts into the woods, when
> nothing matters specially.

('Travelling Between Places', *Little Johnny's Confession*)

LITTLE JOHNNY'S CONFESSION

Little Johnny's Confession was published in a fanfare of publicity that drew attention to Patten's youth. 'Brian Patten is younger than the atom bomb', proclaimed the cover of the first edition somewhat unwisely – perhaps taking its cue from Patten's over-grand subtitle to 'Little Johnny's Foolish Invention': 'A Fable for Atomic Adam'. The image was then further recycled by Allen Ginsberg in his own dust-jacket tribute, which declared Patten's poetry to be 'real magnanimity worded by an Atomic Adam'. Edward Lucie-Smith, editor of *The Liverpool Scene*, was also quoted:

In his work, Brian Patten has been able to get at and describe an entirely new experience: something which simply isn't there for poets older than he is: something which couldn't exist at any other place or time. The 'Little Johnny' sequence has an amazing and very moving detachment, considering how young the author still is. It's quite a feat for any poet, whatever his age, to tell so much truth so simply.

Some of these claims are excessive, of course. Patten is himself much more realistic about the successes and limitations of his first collection – commenting merely, in an interview with the *Observer* in 1983:

> Looking at some of the earlier work I think to myself that I wouldn't write that now, but I don't dismiss the poet who did write it.

It would be pointless to deny that the poems in *Little Johnny's Confession* were written by a teenager, and that sometimes it shows. The embarrassingly unfunny 'Chief Inspector Patten and the Case of the Brown Thigh' and the awful 'The Astronaut' ('We will take a trip| to the planets inside us| where love is the astronaut...') are ultimately the stuff of school magazines, for example – and both are notably absent from *Grinning Jack*, Patten's later selection of poems drawn from his first five volumes. But it is nevertheless remarkable how few of the poems fall into this category, and how intensely the voice of this 18- or 19-year-old from thirty years ago is still able to draw the reader into his world.

'The Beast', for instance is an extraordinarily powerful poem, all the more impressive given the youth of the poet. Beautifully constructed and hauntingly evocative, its images reminiscent of Jean Cocteau films such as *La Belle et la Bête* (1946) or *Orphée* (1949), it describes the young writer's confrontation with his poetic gift. 'I'd begun to see another side of poetry', Patten has explained. 'Sometimes to hunt the poem one must enter territory that can be unfamiliar and frightening, even dangerous mentally':

> Something that was not there before
> has come through the mirror
> into my room.
>
> It is not such a simple creature
> as first I thought –
> from somewhere it has brought a mischief

that troubles both silence and objects,
and now left alone here
I weave intricate reasons for its arrival.

They disintegrate. Today, in January, with
the light frozen on my window, I hear outside
a million panicking birds, and know even out there

comfort is done with; it has shattered
even the stars, this creature
at last come home to me.

(Little Johnny's Confession / Grinning Jack)

In 'The Beast', in a sense, it is the poem that hunts the poet. The 'creature' crosses through a mirror into the poet's room. It is at one and the same time both a reflection of himself and an uninvited visitor from another, mysterious world – an unknown 'somewhere' – that recognizes no boundaries with this one. As it advances towards the poet, it reveals itself initially only through negatives ('not there before'; 'not such a simple creature'). Waves of 'mischief' pulse tangibly through the silence. We focus on the poet 'left alone' (literally stranded at the centre of his own poem, as it takes shape around him) to face his vocation, to search for 'reasons' to explain it away. The poem holds its breath for an instant. Animation is suspended, just as light is 'frozen' on the window, before the 'creature' is recognized as his own and received into its 'home'. The poet knows that the calm and the certainties of his life have changed irrevocably. The world beyond the window, with its 'panicking' birds and 'shattered' stars, becomes an externalization of his mental turmoil.

Interviewed when he received a Pernod Creative Arts Award for *Little Johnny's Confession* in 1967, Patten described the collection as concerning itself with 'a shrinking of the ignorant innocence'. While 'The Beast' clearly deals with the necessary erosion of one form of innocence – the false assumption that poetry was 'simple' – the collection as a whole takes as its major theme the loss of innocence that accompanies growing older. A number of poems deal very directly with recalling Patten's own (still comparatively recent) childhood – his street, his cinema-going, the people he knew (see chapter 1, pages 1-3). But the most original and striking exploration of themes of childhood and lost innocence occurs in the remarkable 'Little Johnny' sequence with which the collection opens and which focuses, in Patten's words, on 'a child becoming aware of the power authority had over him'.

There are eight 'Little Johnny' poems in the sequence, all of which are also included in *Grinning Jack*. 'Little Johnny's Confession', 'Little Johnny's Foolish Invention', 'Little Johnny's Change of Personality', 'Little Johnny's Final Letter', 'Little Johnny Takes a Trip to Another Planet' and 'Ah Johnny, What When You're Older?' appeared in the first edition of *Little Johnny's Confession*; 'Johnny Learns the Language' and 'Little Johnny's Night Visitor' were added to later editions. The poems were written in Patten's attic at Canning Street, after he had left home, and there is an obvious element of autobiography as the poet looks back, through the alter-ego of 'Johnny', on the childhood and the family – or, more particularly the mother – that he has left behind him. Through the character of 'Johnny', however, he is able successfully to universalize these concerns and also to raise a number of questions about the nature of innocence and the extent to which the state is in any case desirable, if inseparable from ignorance.

The opening of the first poem – *Little Johnny's Confession* – sets the tone:

> This morning
>> being rather young and foolish
>> I borrowed a machinegun my father
>> had left hidden since the war, went out,
>> and eliminated a number of small enemies.
>> Since then I have not returned home.
>
> This morning
>> swarms of police with trackerdogs
>> wander about the city
>> with my description printed
>> on their minds, asking:
>> Have you seen him?
>> he is seven years old,
>> likes Pluto, Mighty Mouse,
>> and Biffo the Bear,
>> have you seen him, anywhere?

The bizarre quality of this opening, with its strange amalgam of violence, humour and pathos – via its gun-toting 7-year-old *Beano*–reading anti-hero – is characteristic of the sequence as a whole. Johnny is as much a victim of his own innocence as the 'small enemies' he has gunned down. He is neither adult nor child. He may in theory have gained entry to the world of adult criminality through his 'borrowed' gun and subsequent shooting spree, but his hiding place is still a playground. Similarly, although he appears initially to speak from the perspective of an experienced adult (pronouncing himself as having been 'rather young and foolish') his language has reverted to a vulnerable and unreflective innocence by the closing lines of the poem:

> The trackerdogs will sniff me out,
> they have my lollypops.

The overall effect is strangely dream-like – reinforced by the 'This morning... This morning... This morning...' structure, which presents images framed by captions, almost like a cartoon strip. (The same device is repeated in 'Little Johnny's Change of Personality', which uses 'This afternoon... This afternoon...' and in 'Little Johnny's Foolish Invention', which begins 'One day... Next morning...'.) The frightening isolation of the narrator is also heightened by the use of the first-person voice, which is again characteristic of most of the sequence. His position is entirely internalized.

'Little Johnny's Final Letter' acts as an interesting point of comparison with 'Little Johnny's Confession'. Again, the poem ends with immobility and pathos (in 'Little Johnny's Confession' the speaker tries 'to work out my next move | but cannot move'; in 'Little Johnny's Final Letter' he sits 'behind the windows growing cold'), although this time the separation from his home and family is voluntary. Little Johnny – his age now unspecified – has 'disguised' himself 'as a man' and left home. The disguise is clearly not complete, however. The voice of the child remains, quite unable to picture a routine that does not begin with a bowl of breakfast cereal served by his mother ('Don't leave my shreddies out'), and the longing for her at the end becomes palpable:

> heard your plea on the radio this morning,
> you sounded sad and strangely old.

Although Johnny's 'Final Letter' has attempted to invert the parent–child relationship with its series of negative imperatives ('Don't worry', 'don't hurry' and so on), his very need to write in the first place has demonstrated his reluctance to abandon it altogether for a life of 'obscurity' in long trousers.

This paradox between the attractions and the terrors of escape is central to both poems. Authority figures stalk the 'Little Johnny' poems to place their restrictions on a child's freedom, from the 'police with trackerdogs' in 'Little Johnny's Confession' to the 'Escaped Children Squad' in 'Little Johnny Takes a Trip to Another Planet'. Yet once these oppressors have been eluded successfully, the sequence demonstrates, there can be no return to innocence if adulthood disappoints. 'Ah Johnny, What When You're Older?', the final poem in the sequence, stands back in horror from its own vision of Johnny in middle age – podgy, with pink shirts, polished shoes, and 'Buttoned up to the neck' with a respectability that has become the ultimate confinement.

Little Johnny, this final poem warns, will never be able to 'board a bus full of schoolchildren' and buy 'a single back to innocence'. The note seems to be one of regret. The collection as a whole, however, is at pains to demonstrate that 'innocence' can ultimately be a delusory state. It is no guarantee of happiness and it is no protection against harm. In 'Little Johnny's Night Visitor', nothing – and certainly not the attempt to conjure up the powers of his beloved superheroes – can protect Little Johnny from domestic brutality as the father/bogey-man figure descends on him:

> Last night
>> I heard him try the door of my bedroom.
>> I heard him cross the room.
>> I locked the sheets,
>> I made the bed into iron.
>> I made myself so tiny he could not find me.

Ironically, it is the home environment rather than the world outside that emerges ultimately through this sequence as the most powerful destroyer of childhood. In 'Johnny Learns the Language', Patten evokes not only the malevolence of 'silences in which | words sneak about like thieves' but also the stultifying effects of a family atmosphere fermenting in misery and disharmony:

> I am learning your language.
> 'Loss', 'Defeat', 'Regret' –
> Without understanding
> You would have these be
> the blueprints for my future.

It is here that we get the first glimpse of the concern with the disabling legacies of childhood unhappiness that was to reappear as a theme in Patten's poetry until its resolution in *Armada*.

NOTES TO THE HURRYING MAN

Little Johnny's Confession closed with 'Travelling Between Places', quoted at the beginning of this chapter. Its successor, *Notes to the Hurrying Man* – subtitled *Poems, Winter '66—Summer '68* – is in many ways a transitional collection.

Patten himself was literally on the move. Some of the poems – 'The Telephonists', 'Seen Through the Trees Behind Which You're Walking' and 'Sad Adam' (which also appear in *Grinning Jack*) and 'It Is Always The Same Image', 'Diary Poem', 'Park Poem' and 'A Raft of Apples' – were written in the Canning Street attic before Patten left Liverpool, and therefore still evoke that city, its streets and its parks (he had been working briefly as a labourer in Sefton Park before the publication of *Little Johnny's Confession*). Others were written in Winchester. He had been visiting a friend there early in 1967, in flight from Liverpool, and had decided on impulse to settle there himself. The art college environment appealed to him. He quickly got to know artists teaching at Winchester School of Art (including the sculptor Heinz Henghes, to whose memory he was later to dedicate *Grave Gossip*) and began to find friends within the student community (which included the young Brian Eno, later to find fame as a musician). The relative isolation of the small cathedral city was also an attraction after the hurly-burly of Liverpool:

> My abiding image of Winchester is of quiet, misty streets and a kind of *Steppenwolf* existence on the edge of things.

Little Johnny's Confession had not been a collection *about* Liverpool. Unlike Henri and McGough, Patten consciously avoided the use of local place names in his writing. However,

35

its world had been unmistakably urban and local to Patten, and had been coloured by a high degree of specificity. There are mentions of brand-names, for instance – such as the Mary Quant dress in 'Maud, 1965' – as well as more generalized references to factories, cafés and office blocks. *Notes to the Hurrying Man*, on the other hand, is both less place-specific and less grounded in realistic physical detail.

Fantasy settings, in particular, are markedly more prevalent than in the earlier work – and have also extended to encompass a wider range of images and associations. In *Little Johnny's Confession*, fantasy settings were generally drawn from children's literature or Saturday film-going. For example, 'Ah Johnny, What When You're Older?' gave us Humphrey Bogart, Alice in Wonderland and Winnie the Pooh in the first ten lines. In *Notes to the Hurrying Man*, however, the fantasy settings are richer, more original and more suggestive. The themes of innocence and discovery first established in *Little Johnny's Confession* are now explored within fables – or 'visionary anecdotes', as the critic Richard Holmes described them in his 1969 review in *The Times* of *Notes to the Hurrying Man*.

Six years later, in the Preface to his children's detective story *Mr Moon's Last Case*, Patten was to write:

> to deny even the possibility of another world is a mistake for it limits the mind. It is necessary at a certain age to put speculations aside and concentrate on realistic information ... but it is also necessary to allow the imagination to remain open and to accept the probability, if not the certainty, of another world.

In *Notes to the Hurrying Man* the fable poems offer glimpses of 'another world', where magic still remains a possibility for people who have retained their sense of wonder. Day-trippers from this world include a talking rocking-horse in a Woolworth's department store who leaves his hoof-print on a store detective's skull as evidence of his existence ('You'd Better Believe Him', also in *Grinning Jack*) and a magician telling strange tales of the 'dragons, elves, star-birds and angels' on a planet near our own ('The Magician'). In both poems, the contrast between people who are imaginative and open to experience and those who are small-minded, mean-spirited and oppressive is given a physical focus. Magic becomes a state of mind. In 'The Magician' rationality is shown to be a barrier to possibilities, a suffocant of the imagination:

> And in that room were some who knew his madness
> larger than their sanity, who held
> blurred memory of equal wonder.
> Locked in their heads spun a similar planet,
> but the air in which it spun was congested.

Other fable poems explore situations in which whole worlds can be seen to collide. In 'The Fawn Dreams of Blond Creatures' the collision is between the natural and the urban, the innocent and the corrupt. A fawn sleeping tranquilly in its forest home, 'drunk' on sunlight, is disturbed during the night by hunters and driven out into the city. It wakes in a bus terminus, the one leaf from the forest that it carried in its fur now 'squashed' symbolically by bus wheels. In 'The Projectionist's Nightmare' – also in *Grinning Jack* – which Patten wrote after visiting an open-air cinema in Italy, the collision of worlds is more violent still:

> A bird finds its way into the cinema,
> finds the beam, flies down it,
> smashes into a screen depicting a garden,
> a sunset and two people being nice to each other.
> Real blood, real intestines slither down
> the likeness of a tree.

Appalled, the audience riots at the splattering of blood and guts across their celluloid sunset. Here, ironically, it is reality and not fantasy that is being viewed as a form of pornography. Moreover, 'slither' is not only a marvellously tactile word, suggesting a horrible lumpen stickiness making agonizingly slow progress down the screen, but it also invites the reader to picture the intestines physically as snakes, and therefore to make an instinctive association with the serpent in the Garden of Eden.

Almost all of Patten's 'visionary anecdotes' draw strongly on imagery derived from nature and the animal world, and the animals in his fables often also take on a symbolic or allegorical significance. One association firmly established in *Notes to the Hurrying Man* (following on from 'Song of the Pink Bird' and 'The Fruitful Lady of Dawn' in *Little Johnny's Confession*) is the association between bird song and poetry, and therefore

37

between the bird and the poet (in 'The Song', for example, and in 'The Lyric Bird', both of which also appear in *Grinning Jack*). In itself, this is obviously something of a commonplace in poetry, although it is interesting to trace Patten's subsequent manipulation of the image (in 'The Literary Gathering' in *The Irrelevant Song*, for examples – see page 44). Other animals, however, carry a wider range of possible associations – such as the strange little creature described in what has become one of the best known of Patten's early poems:

> I've found a small dragon in the woodshed,
> Think it must have come from deep inside a forest
> because it's damp and green and leaves
> are still reflecting in its eyes.

('A Small Dragon')

Here, the handling of the symbol is both exquisite and complex. The dragon is beautiful, but timid. Although as a dragon – even a small one – it might be expected to breathe fire (and its nest 'among the coal' reminds us of this), this dragon is silent and forlorn. It rejects the delicacies of 'roots of stars, hazelnut and dandelion' with which the speaker tries to tempt it, and its luminous eyes beg dumbly for something that he does not know how to provide. The dragon is fascinating to him, though unfamiliar and 'out of place' in his world. He feels 'wonder', but also uncertainty over whether he dare share the dragon with the 'you' of the poem. The 'small dragon' comes from the world of the imagination, and ultimately it becomes a symbol of something special and private that he nevertheless wants to share – possibly his poetry, perhaps even his love:

> If you believed in it I would come
> hurrying to your house to let you share my wonder
> but I want instead to see
> if you yourself will pass this way.

'A Small Dragon' was later to be included in Patten's collection of *Love Poems*, as were a number of poems from *Notes to the Hurrying Man*. Increasingly, love begins to emerge as a dominant theme. The transitional nature of this collection is again worth stressing. In *Little Johnny's Confession* – apart from the starkly moving 'Song for Last Year's Wife' (also published in *Love Poems*) – love poetry often took the form of descriptive and mostly urban cameos, such as 'Party Piece'. In *Notes to the Hurrying Man* Patten's canvas broadens. The range of experiences evoked is now more varied and multi-layered. New themes, such as ageing, begin to be developed.

The structuring of the poems also starts to become more sophisticated – particularly through the handling of narrative perspective. In a number of poems, for instance, the narrator is describing and commenting on a situation both from within the situation and from beyond it. The poems therefore become almost like a set of Chinese boxes, with the emotions at the centre of the poem also encased, as it were, by first internal and then external perspectives on the situation.

'You Come To Me Quiet As Rain Not Yet Fallen' (also published in *Love Poems*) provides a particularly fine example of Patten's ability in this respect. It was written shortly after his arrival in Winchester (on the same day as 'A Small Dragon' and 'Into My Mirror Has Walked'), and it focuses on the fears and insecurities of an older woman approaching her younger lover, who is the narrator of the poem. It opens as follows:

> You come to me quiet as rain not yet fallen
> afraid of how you might fail yourself your
> dress seven summers old is kept open
> in memory of sex, smells warm, of boys,
> and of the once long grass.
> But we are colder now; we have not
> love's first magic here. You come to me
> quiet as bulbs not yet broken
> out into sunlight.
>
> The fear I see in your now lining face
> changes to puzzlement when my hands reach
> for you as branches reach. Your dress
> does not fall easily, nor does your body
> sing of its own accord. What love added to
> a common shape no longer seems a miracle.
> You come to me with your age wrapped in excuses
> and afraid of its silence.

The action of the poem could hardly be simpler. The man takes off the woman's dress, and they will begin to make love. The dress has been charged explicitly with the smells of sex in the long grass, and anticipation is heightened as the poem slows down the action to focus, film-like, first on the woman's face and then on the speaker's hands. But this is no ordinary strip-show. The woman's face is lined, and she is afraid. The final removal of her dress is awkward. And the reader is disturbingly aware that, once unclothed, she has been stripped of all defences. The dress in which she had 'wrapped' herself was a symbol of her younger self – vibrant, confident in her sexual desirability. Now the dress is gone, there is no hiding from the reality of a body that is ageing or her terror that she is no longer attractive. Both physically and emotionally she has been laid bare.

'You Come To Me Quiet As Rain Not Yet Fallen' is a powerfully compassionate poem. Although it is narrated by the man, the reader's sympathies are still very much engaged by the woman who has made herself so vulnerable to scrutiny. The manipulation of perspective referred to above is masterly. The separate viewpoints of both the woman and the man are depicted equally sympathetically, even though the woman is seen entirely through the eyes of the man. In addition, the 'us' of the final stanza ('now those shapes terrify most | that remind *us* of our own') and the 'our' of the last line ('the last of *our* senses closing') suggest a further, universal 'we' that goes beyond the two people in the poem. Most of us are afraid of ageing, Patten reminds us, because most of us are afraid of dying. The encapsulation of differing perspectives of time within the poem's structure is also effective. The time-frame of the poem includes past, present and future simultaneously. In the final stanza, the past of the couple's 'younger lives' is superimposed onto the present of 'this bed and room' and finally projected into the future as the woman looks out 'across years'.

Natural imagery is important in this poem, particularly imagery drawn from the seasons. For example, the images of rainfall and new bulbs in the first stanza associate the woman's hesitant expectancy with the spring that, poignantly, she will never be able to recapture. Many other of the love poems in *Notes to the Hurrying Man* similarly relate states of mind to the natural world. The use of imagery drawn from winter to denote an internal landscape of emotions that have petrified is made explicit, for instance, in 'Diary Poem':

> Confined by faith to a flower that's perishing
> we move, frozen not by these seasons
> but by our own weather...

Here, the fusion of image and emotion is precise, focused and effective. 'You Come To Me Quiet As Rain Not Yet Fallen' also succeeds magnificently in mingling its physical location – the bedroom – with a suggested landscape of flowers and trees. Occasionally, however, some of the love poems in *Notes to the Hurrying Man* are weakened rather than strengthened by their willingness to wander too far into the 'other world' that gives the volume as a whole its particular character. By and large, fantasy settings prove to function less effectively in the poems that are primarily about feelings than in fables, where a narrative predominates. For example, the imaginary forest in 'Arriving in Winter' – where the narrator finds an angel's body that foreshadows the death of a relationship – is over-complex, over-written and ultimately a distraction. The reader is too busy struggling through the allegory to remain in touch with the emotion. We can't see the poem for the trees.

Crucially, Patten not only recognized this potential flaw in *Notes to the Hurrying Man* but sensibly provided an antidote in the form of the excellent 'Ode on Celestial Music':

> 'Ode on Celestial Music' was one of the last poems I wrote for the collection. I was getting worried about the poetry – that it might be starting to get too abstract, too quasi-mystical. I needed to bring it back to earth, to ground it again.

'Ode on Celestial Music' brings its crusty protagonist down to earth with a bump. Indeed, the poem ends with him crouching on his floor with his ear to the floorboards. He has demanded only the purest, most esoteric form of lyrical expression – celestial music, which alone will herald perfect harmony and happiness. He has dismissed the seductively beautiful singing of his neighbour in the bathroom below as a worthless earthly imitation of the music of the spheres. As the girl sings, something just as magical as the celestial music he longs for is in motion. But he dismisses the flowers that are growing up towards him through her bathroom ceiling as a 'filthy trick', literally cutting himself off from the experience with his scissors. He has destroyed the flowers and ended the song:

It's not celestial music it's the girl in the bathroom singing.
You can tell. Although it's winter
the trees outside her window have grown leaves,
all manner of flowers push up through the floorboards.
I think – what a filthy trick that is to play on me,
I snip them with my scissors shouting
'I want only bona fide celestial music!'
Hearing this she stops singing.

Primarily, of course, this poem is an allegory about the writing and reception of poetry. Certainly, that is the dimension to which Larkin was responding when he likened Patten's hostile critics, suspicious and scornful of a different form of poetry, to the 'scissor-men' (see chapter 2, page 24). And, interestingly, when the poem was republished in *Grinning Jack*, Patten replaced the word 'flower' in the last line with the word 'song'. But one can also see that – despite its own dimension of fantasy – the poem is arguing forcefully for a celebration of what is ordinary and real (here, a smiling girl in a slipping bath towel) rather than an over-extravagant reaching out for the stars. This insight was to have a bearing on the transcendent clarity of the language of Patten's later love poetry.

THE IRRELEVANT SONG AND *VANISHING TRICK*

These two collections taken together probably represent Patten's finest and certainly his most sustained achievement as a love poet. Other avenues still remained to be explored by him in the future and his poetry was to take important new directions, as this study will show. But the collections nevertheless form a vital landing stage, as it were, in his poetic development.

The two volumes were not written with the intention of forming a cycle. However, since *The Irrelevant Song* (published in 1971) celebrates the beginning of a love affair and *Vanishing Trick* (published in 1976) reflects on its ending, it is perhaps inevitable that they have come to be viewed in this way. Together, the two collections encompass a number of poems that have quite rightly become modern-day classics. And *Vanishing Trick* in particular demonstrates a new certainty, authority and confidence in its control of a markedly sparer poetic style.

Reviewing the collection in *Tribune* in 1976, Martin Booth commented that:

> Patten has emerged with this new collection into a fully matured talent, taking on the intricacies of love and beauty with a totally new approach, new for him and contemporary poetry ... Of his generation, he is the master poet of his genre, the only one continually and successfully to 'ring true'.

Patten was still 'travelling between places' when he worked on these collections. In 1970 he had left Winchester for London and rented a room in Notting Hill Gate, west London. He already knew the area, since he had frequently had occasion to travel to London from Winchester during his time there – often for social events, such as the fashionable pop party satirized in 'Party Notes' in *Notes to the Hurrying Man* where VIP guests had included the Rolling Stones. A number of other writers and artists were already living in Notting Hill Gate, round by the bustling Portobello Road market – an area that was much shabbier then than now but had already acquired a reputation as a lively and fashionably bohemian community. Patten was soon at home there. Then, in the same year, he met Mary Moore – daughter of the sculptor Henry Moore – at a party. Their first meeting is described in 'Early in the Evening' in *The Irrelevant Song / Love Poems*:

> I met her early in the evening
> The cars were going home
> I was twenty-four and dreaming ...

They fell in love, and began a relationship that was to continue until 1975.

For most of the five-year relationship Patten and Mary Moore lived together in Holland Park, a rather smarter part of west London than Notting Hill Gate – although they also spent time at a farmhouse near her parents' house in Much Hadham in Hertfordshire as well as at the Moores' holiday home in Tuscany, and later at a house Mary Moore bought nearby. It was a happy and productive period for both of them. Herself a talented artist, Mary Moore collaborated with Patten as illustrator of the children's books he wrote at that time – *Jumping Mouse, Mr Moon's Last Case* and *Emma's Doll* – and her gentle, wistful images are widely credited with enhancing the success of those books. In the winter of 1975 the relationship ended, and Patten moved back to Notting Hill Gate, where most of the poems in *Vanishing Trick* were written.

Patten has always been concerned to stress that his love poetry should not necessarily be read autobiographically. Critics and reporters have scratched their heads needlessly, for example, over what family secret might lie behind the title of 'Song For Last Year's Wife' in *Little Johnny's Confession / Love Poems*. (Patten has never married, in fact.) The inspiration for any of his love poetry, according to Patten:

> need not be one individual, or even a woman I've personally known. Sometimes the lovers are observed friends. Sometimes a single poem may bring two or three different experiences together.

This point still applies to both *The Irrelevant Song* and *Vanishing Trick*. The poems are not all directed to or derived from one person, nor should they be read as an autobiographical sequence. But it is nevertheless clear that they are among the most personal of Patten's love poems, particularly those appearing in *Vanishing Trick*.

Unlike *Vanishing Trick*, which is almost exclusively concerned with love poetry and is remarkably even and consistent in tone, *The Irrelevant Song* includes poems covering a variety of themes and adopting a range of forms and stances. For example, a poem such as 'Interruption at the Opera House' – from which the mime-artist Lindsay Kemp created a mime – continues the tradition of the urban fable established in *Notes to the Hurrying Man*. In that poem, a contrast is drawn between the privileged purchasers of culture – 'the rich and famous' in their 'quietly expensive boxes' – and 'the rightful owner of the music', a caged canary. At the end of the poem, the 'fur-wrapped crowds' have left the opera-house in confusion, and the bird sings on to the attendants, their families and their children, who are hailed as 'the rightful owners of the song.' It is a charming enough poem, an allegory on the place of poetry in a similar vein to 'Ode on Celestial Music', but it is hardly ground-breaking – although it is interesting that in 'The Literary Gathering' (also in *Grinning Jack*) Patten himself has become a canary whose new cage (among the literary intelligentsia) does not 'suit' him. Similarly, although 'The Literary Gathering' itself – along with 'The

Irrelevant Song' ('A Pantomime of Kinds' written in response to Wordsworth's 'Ode: Intimations of Immortality') and 'Albatross Ramble' (with its allusion to Coleridge's 'The Rime of the Ancient Mariner') – signals in this volume a more explicit interest in overtly 'literary' themes and in the work of other authors than was apparent in *Notes to the Hurrying Man*, there is no major development at this stage. Patten did not choose to return to these topics until *Grave Gossip* and *Storm Damage*.

In its love poetry, though, *The Irrelevant Song* attains new levels of emotional clarity. The poems achieve a striking simplicity of expression that is grounded not in the conscious celebration of innocence that can be both an attraction and a weakness of his earlier work but in a wisdom born of experience. Images are sharper, language is purer. Patten's warning to himself in 'Ode on Celestial Music' against possible over-embellishment has been taken triumphantly to heart. 'Through All Your Abstract Reasoning' – a poem that takes as its own thesis the contrast between the self-protection afforded by abstract speculation and the nerve-tingling immediacy of direct experience – begins gently, and utterly simply. Not a word is wasted, and the pace is beautifully controlled. Slowly the landscape and setting unfurl, the phrases rolling on from comma to comma as the traveller makes his way across the open fields. Then suddenly, the poem – like the reader – jolts abruptly to a temporary standstill as a pang of realization strikes:

> Coming back one evening through deserted fields
> when the birds, drowsy with sleep,
> have all but forgotten you,
> you stop, and for one moment jerk alive.
>
> Something has passed through you
> that alters and enlightens: O
> realisation of what has gone and was real.

> *(The Irrelevant Song / Love Poems)*

Several of the love poems in *The Irrelevant Song* focus on moments of realization. 'Poem Written in the Street on a Rainy Evening', which also appears in *Love Poems*, joins Wordsworth's 'I Wandered Lonely as a Cloud' as one of the few lyrics in the English language able to communicate and recreate the exhilaration of a moment of unrestrained joy. Wordsworth's heart 'dances' with the remembered fluttering of his glorious 'host' of daffodils. Patten's heart zig-zags gaily through an imagined night sky:

> Everything I lost was found again.
> I tasted wine in my mouth.
> My heart was like a firefly; it moved
> Through the darkest objects laughing.

The intensity of the experience is deeply sensuous. There is wine in the poet's mouth. The world has become a banquet:

> A feast was spread; a world
> was suddenly made edible.
> And there was forever to taste it.

In 'At Four O'Clock in the Morning' Patten again succeeds in evoking the immediacy of a single moment through the verbal control and precision of expression that is so characteristic of the finest poetry in this volume. It is a poem of extraordinary resonance:

> As all is temporary and is changeable,
> So in this bed my love you lie,
> Temporary beyond imagining;
> Trusting and certain, in present time you rest,
> A world completed.
>
> Yet already are the windows freaked with dawn;
> Shrill song reminds
> Each of a separate knowledge;
> Shrill light might make of love
> A weight both false and monstrous.
>
> So hush; enough words are used:
> We know how blunt can grow such phrases as
> Only children use without
> Awareness of their human weight.
>
> There is no need to impose upon feelings
> Yesterday's echo.
> I love you true enough;
> Beyond this, nothing is expected.

> (*The Irrelevant Song / Love Poems*)

The crafting of the poem is clearly conscious, drawing evocatively on literary allusion to lend universality and weight to its central mood and thought. Most notably it weaves in echoes of W. H. Auden's well known poem 'Lullaby', which begins:

> Lay your sleeping head my love
> Human on my faithless arm;

Both poets use a similar situation – a lover contemplating his sleeping partner – to weigh the happiness of the moment against a grave but uncomplaining awareness of the uncertainty of the future. For Auden, 'certainty' and 'fidelity' will pass 'on the stroke of midnight'; for Patten, 'shrill' birdsong and the light of morning – also given an aural dimension and a jarring discordancy through the adjective 'shrill' – herald the invasion of a new dawn that might bring the idyll to an end. But the tone of both poems is one of calm and acceptance. Both poems address the sleeping partner gently, almost like a child who should not be frightened with this new knowledge (Auden's poem is itself a 'lullaby'; Patten's poem whispers 'hush'). And both acknowledge as inevitable – and therefore without anger or resentment – the frailty of all human beings (Auden's stress in the second line of his poem on 'Human' is echoed in Patten's 'Awareness of their human weight').

Patten's poem is more immediately domestic than Auden's, with its bed, its window and the glimpse of a world beyond that window. He does not seek to people the poem further – whereas Auden's poem becomes progressively more crowded with hermits, 'fashionable madmen' and card-readers. Patten's focus remains close, and the intimacy of the last lines is therefore deeply moving. The diction is simple and accessible (although some critics have noted the unusual word 'freaked' as a possible echo from Robert Graves's poem 'Three Songs for the Lute'). But it is interesting to note that the poem's gravity and dignity in the face of a world that is 'temporary and changeable' is both reflected in and intensified by a certain heightening of language. The word ordering, for example, is far from colloquial and serves to lend a weight of seriousness to the sentiments. The second line, for instance, demands a slow and deliberate reading, and inversions such as 'already are the windows freaked' and 'how blunt can grow such phrases' give an almost proverbial authority.

In *Vanishing Trick*, the transience of love has proved itself to be not merely a possibility but a reality. The volume opens with 'A Love Poem' (retitled 'Whose Body Has Opened' in *Love Poems*), a bravely naked and erotic evocation of the comforts and certainties which love can seem to offer:

> – whose body has opened
> Night after night
> Harbouring loneliness,
> Cancelling the doubts
> Of which I am made,
> Night after night
> Taste me upon you.

The rest of the collection traces the harrowing cycle of emotions that follows the unwelcome confirmation that such certainties are in the end illusory – and that 'loneliness' and 'doubts' cannot always be harboured or cancelled as permanently as one might wish.

The prevailing tone of *Vanishing Trick*, as in *The Irrelevant Song*'s 'At Four O'Clock in the Morning', is one of sadness and of resignation rather than of anger:

> There do not have to be reasons for such changes,
> there do not have to be.
> In the morning bodies evaporate and nothing
> can quite hold them together.
>
> ('Vanishing Trick', also in *Love Poems*)

But the poems are nevertheless painfully specific in their depiction of the breakdown of a love affair and of the searing emptiness that can follow in its wake. The diction of the collection as a whole is most characteristically simple, elegiac, and solemn – even biblical – in its repetitions:

> You lose your love for her and then
> It is her who is lost,
> And then it is both who are lost
>
> ('And Nothing is Ever As Perfect As You Want It To Be', also in *Love Poems*)

> And sometimes it happens that you are friends and then
> You are not friends,
> And friendship has passed.
> And whole days are lost and among them

A fountain empties itself.

And sometimes it happens that you are loved and then
You are not loved,
And love is past.
And whole days are lost and among them
A fountain empties itself into the grass.

('Sometimes It Happens', also in *Love Poems*)

However, there are nevertheless moments when the language becomes almost physical in its grief. In 'Simple Lyric', which ends with an anguished expression of powerlessness, deprivation and loss have become a form of physical as well as emotional suffocation:

She is away and I cannot breathe her in.
I am ill simply through wanting her.

(also in *Love Poems*)

'The Assassination of the Morning', which is also published in *Love Poems*, opens with an extraordinary image that reverberates like the bewildered howl of an injured animal:

The morning has a hole in its side,
It rolls through the grass like a wounded bear,
Over and over it goes, clutching its wound,
Its wound fat with sorrow.

This translation of feeling into object form is a further new departure for Patten in this volume. In an essay on *Hamlet* published in 1919, the poet T. S. Eliot described the technique as the finding of the 'objective correlative':

The only way of expressing emotion in the form of art is by finding an 'objective correlative'; in other words, a set of objects, a situation, a chain of events which shall be the formula of that *particular* emotion; such as that when the external facts, which must terminate in sensory experience, are given, the emotion is immediately evoked.

In 'Vanishing Trick', pain is given a particularly memorable physical shape through the 'objective correlative' of a row of razors in a bathroom:

Now in the bathroom the razors wait like a line of little friends,
they glow as much as roses,
they glow, glow with pain, with their own electricity,
they glow with darkness.

49

Here the verse form embraces a domestic register and an insistent urgency of tone that is strongly reminiscent of Sylvia Plath's *Ariel* poems (Faber and Faber, 1965). Light and dark become indistinguishable. Death becomes an inviting possibility, charged with unnerving eroticism.

Crucially, however – and unlike Plath's *Ariel* poems – both the poem 'Vanishing Trick' and the collection as a whole reject the seductive 'glow' of morbidity and the attractions of self pity. Ultimately, the process of grieving for lost love in *Vanishing Trick* leads to a courageous and affirmative conclusion. Reviewing the collection in *The Times Literary Supplement* in 1976, D. M. Thomas described it as:

> a truthful and tender sequence of love poems, or poems about the death of love; but it is also about the drive into oneself, that painful lonely experience involving the shedding of false images of oneself created by other people.

In *Vanishing Trick*, the outcome of this 'drive' into the self is the turning-point of realization that just as human love endures from generation to generation, surviving and transcending all individual loss, so individual loss is also survivable – and may even, as an experience, prove strengthening. In that sense, the volume becomes finally one of celebration.

'You Missed the Sunflowers at Their Height' (also in *Love Poems*) is one of the collection's key poems in this respect. It is an assured and moving poem, again striking in its simplicity:

> You missed the sunflowers at their height,
> Came back when they were bent and worn
> And the gnats, half-froze, fell one by one
> Into the last of the sprawling marigolds.
>
> And as if linked to some spider thread
> Made visible only because of rain,
> You sat and watched the day come light
> And hope leapt back into your brain,
>
> And suddenly this surprising earth
> No longer clouded, was known again,
> And all you had thought lost you found
> Was simply for a time mislaid.

Appropriately for a poem demonstrating that love and hope are perennial, the imagery draws on cycles from the natural world.

Sunflowers and marigolds may flourish and then die, but implicit in the poem is the fact that they will flower again. Gnats have their season, but the species will continue. Sun follows cloud and rain. This theme of continuity is reinforced by the poem's verse form, driven inexorably forward by the repetition of 'And' and by rhymes lacing from stanza to stranza as unobtrusively as the poem's own 'spider thread'. 'Height' and 'light' link the first stanza and the second; 'rain', 'brain', and 'again' link the second stanza and the third. Moreover, the simple repeated four-line verse structure and iambic metre of the three stanzas are also effective in lending an atmosphere of timelessness. They link the poem, for example, to the lyrics of Blake or of Wordsworth – a link that is further intensified by verbal echo. Cycles of allusion bind the poem. Patten's sunflowers recall Blake's 'Ah, Sunflower! weary of time'. 'Hope leapt back' recalls Wordsworth's 'My heart leaps up when I behold| A rainbow in the sky'. And the formula 'this...earth' possibly even carries Shakespearean echoes, recalling 'this earth of majesty' and 'this earth, this realm' from *Richard II*, as well as 'this goodly frame, the earth' from *Hamlet*. More powerfully still, the poem also recalls verbally its own predecessor, 'Poem Written in the Street on a Rainy Evening' in *The Irrelevant Song* (see page 45). The effect is persuasive and uplifting. The cycle of discovery, loss and rediscovery that these two volumes together celebrate has been brought full circle.

A further impressive strength of *Vanishing Trick* – again arguably differentiating it from a collection such as Plath's *Ariel* – is its admirable lack of ego on the part of the poet and its genuine independence from personal context. Although many of the poems *are* personal, as has been noted, this is not a confessional volume describing situations or sets of circumstances that are uniquely individual to the poet. It is not a book about the ending of Patten's own love affair. Rather, it resonates for the reader because it describes through example the ending of all love affairs. It is perhaps of biographical interest to know that the fountain in 'Sometimes It Happens' is the fountain in Holland Park in London, near where Patten had lived with Mary Moore. But it is of no consequence to an understanding and appreciation of the poem. The poem is universal.

'One Another's Light', which closed the original collection

51

and is also published in *Love Poems*, is another example of a poem that had a very specific stimulus. It was written several weeks after Patten and Mary Moore had separated, and they had met again by chance at a crowded party at the artist David Hockney's vast flat in Notting Hill Gate. Yet the poem that resulted makes no specific allusion to the precise setting or context of the experience described. Instead, it brings to an effective and affecting conclusion the strain of imagery associated with light that had been established initially in *Notes to the Hurrying Man*, in poems such as 'Doubt Shall Not Make An End of You' which ends with the following lines:

> Feel nothing separate then,
> we have translated each other into light
> and into love go streaming.

(also in Love Poems)

As Patten was later to explain in an interview with the *Liverpool Daily Post* in 1981, the notion of intimacy in his poetry is often expressed in terms of an interchange of light:

> I think that we are all caught up in each other's lives. In one another's light... It's to do with the way people influence each other. I think the light which I talk about in the poems is often about a kind of clarity... how sometimes the world seems suddenly a little bit brighter for no apparent reason.

In 'One Another's Light' this image triumphantly universalizes the poem. The permanent, positive effect of being illuminated by another person and of having 'left a mark' or 'wrought| Some kind of charm or spell', however 'briefly', on someone else's life and future is recognized as a life-enhancing privilege:

> It's hard to guess what brought me here,
> Away from where I've hardly been and now
> Am never likely to go again.
>
> Faces are lost, and places passed
> At which I could have stopped
> And stopping, been glad enough.
>
> Some faces left a mark;
> And I on them might have wrought
> Some kind of charm or spell
> To make their futures work,

But it's hard to guess
How one thing on another
Works an influence.
We pass –
And lit briefly by one another's light
Think the way we go is right.

(also in *Love Poems*)

4

The Skeleton in Everyone: Poems 1979–1988

> I saw the skeleton in everyone
> And noticed how it walked in them
>
> ('Staring at the Crowd', *Grave Gossip* / *Grinning Jack*)

GRAVE GOSSIP AND *STORM DAMAGE*

Vanishing Trick marked a watershed in Patten's poetry, confirming and securing his reputation as a love poet of vision and distinction. Over the years of *Grave Gossip* (1979) and *Storm Damage* (1988), however, his focus as a writer was subtly to begin to shift – even though love was still to remain an important theme in his future poetry collections. In the decade that followed *Vanishing Trick*, Patten himself was growing older, friends and family were growing older alongside him, friends were beginning to die. The themes of ageing and of mortality, as the title quotation suggests, began to feature more prominently in his work.

The years of *Grave Gossip* and *Storm Damage* were in many ways an important time for re-evaluation. The metaphor of being lost in the woods which appears in both 'Frogs in the Wood' and 'Going Back and Going On' in *Grave Gossip* / *Grinning Jack* signals a search not only for personal but also for artistic direction. Ultimately this period was to function as a time of experiment and rehearsal. *Grave Gossip* and *Storm Damage* can be seen with hindsight to have foreshadowed and led up to the publication of *Armada* (1996), just as *Little Johnny's Confession*, *Notes to the Hurrying Man* and – to some extent – *The Irrelevant Song* can be seen now to have blazed the trail that was to reach its destination in *Vanishing Trick*.

During the time in which he was writing the poems in *Grave Gossip*, Patten was still based in London – although by then he had moved from Notting Hill Gate to a basement flat in Holland Park Gardens – but he was spending substantial time away from the city living in a boathouse in Devon on the country estate of Sharpham owned by the philosopher Maurice Ash, who had been a friend of Patten's for some years. The affectionate birthday poem 'Dear Maurice' in *Storm Damage* was written for Maurice Ash. Patten still remains a frequent visitor to the Sharpham estate and to Devon's South Hams area, where a number of friends such as Val and Jim Hennessy have since settled. (Val Hennessy, as Literary Editor of the *Daily Mail*, has been a long-time champion of the Liverpool Poets.) 'One Reason for Sympathy' (also published in *Grinning Jack*) was written at the boathouse, as were 'Going Back and Going On' and 'Frogs in the Wood', which are mentioned briefly above. The wood referred to in the latter two poems is Sharpham Wood itself.

Grave Gossip is not devoted as wholly to death and dying as its title might imply. In fact, its original draft title was *Telephones and Grave Gossip*, and poems such as 'The Wrong Number' and 'I Studied Telephones Constantly' continue the fascination with telephones as a metaphor for communication (or its limitations) which was established initially in *Notes to the Hurrying Man* through 'The Telephonists' and 'Making a Call' (all of these 'telephone' poems except 'Making a Call' are also published in *Grinning Jack*). In addition, as noted earlier (see chapter 3, page 45), *The Irrelevant Song* had signalled an interest in literary burlesque that is revisited in this volume. 'Trapped (1)' and 'Trapped (2)' conjure up the imagined horrors and dilemmas of overnight incarceration in the Poetry Society and Cornell University library vaults respectively – among *'illustrious ghosts'* in 'Trapped (1)' and 'literary remains' in 'Trapped (2)'. Unfortunately, however, neither effort is especially funny – nor, later, was 'A Falible [sic] Lecture' on English Literature in *Storm Damage* – and it is interesting, not to say something of a relief, that Patten has subsequently abandoned this particular avenue. Similarly, a flurry of experiments with a 'Brer Rabbit' character (in 'Brer Rabbit's Howler', which also appears in *Grinning Jack*, the luckless rabbit commits the social gaffe of turning up to a ball with a baby's foot proudly attached to the lapel of his best suit) failed to yield a naïve anti-hero comparable in richness and complexity to Patten's own 'Little Johnny' creation (see chapter 3, pages 31-5).

However, in the meditations and variations on the theme of dying that constitute the majority of its poems and give the volume its characteristic tone, *Grave Gossip* signals already a number of the interests and concerns that were later to achieve richer, more evocative and more complete expression in *Armada*. In 'Friends', for example, which is published in significantly altered form in *Grinning Jack*, contemplation of redundant entries in an address book leads to meditation on the randomness of people's dates of dying:

> Then I learned how the exodus from this place
> Is not scheduled,
> At times the young leave before the old
> And the old
> Are left gaping at their fortune.
> . . . .
> Looking back through an address book containing
> The names they have abandoned
> I realise that as from today
> I haven't fingers enough to count
> The graves in which they are exiled.

(Interestingly, *Armada*'s closing poem, 'The Brackets', also takes a book as its stimulus – in this case the contents page of a poetry anthology, where poets' birth and death dates are listed in brackets – and contemplates death's resolute imperviousness to any human notions of fair play. The later poem, however, attains an emotive (and a visual) dimension that was lacking in 'Friends', as well as acquiring – through its essentially literary context – a degree of depth and specificity. In 'The Brackets' the dates of Wilfred Owen, Patten's boyhood hero (see chapter 1, page 4) who died in combat at 25, are ruefully compared with the dates of Robert Graves (1895–1985), who had also fought in the First World War and whom Patten had known personally from the sixties, when he first visited the Graves family at their home in Deia, on the north coast of Majorca. Patten himself therefore becomes the surviving link between the two at this stage, a temporary point of continuity in the chain of life and death:

> At first it seems unfair,
> Twenty-five, then gone. Hard to believe
> I drank beneath the stars with one
> Who crouched beneath the light from flak with him...)

Grave Gossip's 'Friends' is dedicated in *Grinning Jack* to a London neighbour Liz Kylle and to the poet Harry Fainlight, both friends of Patten's who had died young. (Patten considers Harry Fainlight, brother of the poet Ruth Fainlight, to have been 'one of the greatest unsung lyrical poets of the twentieth century'.) *Grave Gossip* includes a number of poems to named people – including, in 'John Poole's Bullying the Angels', a cheerfully irreverent memoir of a particularly difficult and alarming man remembered from Patten's Winchester days who is depicted 'strolling towards Paradise| in a threatening sort of way' (the poem is also published in *Grinning Jack*). As previously mentioned, the volume as a whole is dedicated to Heinz Henghes, a sculptor friend – also from Winchester (see chapter 3, page 35) – who had died prematurely and last visited Patten in London in the early seventies to give him some etchings. He had not mentioned his illness, but the two had had a conversation about Patten's children's book *Jumping Mouse* that becomes the epigraph of 'The Last Gift':

> H.H. *'What's the story about?'*
> B.P. *'About a mouse that gets eaten by an eagle.'*
> H.H. *'Poor mouse.'*
> B.P. *'No, the mouse becomes part of the eagle.'*
> H.H. *'Lucky mouse. Perhaps I'll be that lucky.'*

'The Last Gift', which also appears in *Grinning Jack*, is a thoughtful and tender poem, imagining Henghes's reincarnation via 'the blood or the tongue of a sparrow' or 'the scent of a foxglove' or as a 'moth with no memory of flame'. It contemplates movingly the mixed feelings of survivors, gifted for no reasons that are obvious to them with a longer span of existence than those they mourn:

> And now as one by dreamless one they are dropped
> Into the never distant, dreamless grave,
> As individual memory fades
> And eye-bewildering light is put aside,
> We grow more baffled by this last
> Gift of the days they are denied.

As indicated above, this theme of disparity of life-span was to re-emerge in *Armada* in poems such as 'The Brackets'. More importantly, however, the exploration of the experience of mourning that is begun here was also to continue – culminating in its authoritative refinement in *Armada*'s classic 'So Many Different Lengths of Time', a poem so distinctive in its vision that it ultimately borrows little other than the word 'baffled' from the earlier work (see chapter 5, pages 68–9).

Of poems to named people, the most assured of the elegies in *Grave Gossip* – indeed, probably the finest poem in the collection – is undoubtedly 'Blake's Purest Daughter', a lyrical tribute to the poet Stevie Smith that celebrates her as one of William Blake's 'Daughters of Albion'. Patten had read with Smith on a number of occasions, including at the Poetry Gala at the Royal Festival Hall in 1969 (see chapter 1, page 11) and – three years earlier – at a reading at the Palais des Beaux Arts in Brussels. He retained a great fondness for her, as well as an admiration for her work (as is also demonstrated in 'The Critics' Chorus' in the same collection, quoted previously in chapter 2, page 25). 'Blake's Purest Daughter' retains the simplicity of expression and control of form perfected in *Vanishing Trick,* and its tone is both heightened and dignified by the stately repetitions of the question and answer format as the speaker interrogates each of the elements in turn. It is a beautifully crafted poem, moving elegantly and persuasively from uncertainty to affirmation:

> Must she always walk with Death, must she?
> I went out and asked the sky.
> No, it said, no,
> She'll do as I do, as I do.
> I go on forever.
>
> Must she always walk with Death, must she?
> I went and asked the soil.
> No, it said, no,
> She'll do as I do, as I do.
> I will nourish her forever.
>
> Must she always walk with Death, must she?
> I listened to the water.
> No, it said, no.
> She'll do as I do, as I do.
> I will cleanse her forever.

Must she always walk with Death, must she?
I went and asked the fire.
No, said the fire,
She'll burn as I burn, as I burn.
She will be in brilliance forever.

O but I am not Death, said Death slyly,
I am only no longer living,
Only no longer knowing exorbitant grief.
Do not fear me, so many share me.

Stevie elemental
Free now of the personal,
Through sky and soil
And fire and water
Swim on, Blake's purest daughter!

(also in *Grinning Jack*)

Following the publication of *Grave Gossip*, there was a gap of
nine years before *Storm Damage* was published, although
Penguin issued *New Volume*, a companion volume to *The Mersey
Sound* featuring new work by all three Liverpool Poets, in 1983.
In the interim between the two collections, Patten had been
publishing extensively and highly successfully for children (see
Afterword, pages 75–81) and had also undertaken national and
international tours. Over the winter of 1984–5, for example, he
gave a reading tour of Indian universities. In the meantime, he
had bought and moved to a house in London's Brook Green in
1983, acquired a phlegmatic black cat – Wiz – who was later to
inspire *Armada*'s lovely 'Inessential Things', and begun regularly
to revisit the Graves family in Deia after a break of some years.
The discontented couple in 'The Package' – arguing 'beneath
the hotel's vine' and bitter not only about the stormy weather
that has blighted their planned holiday but also about the
metaphorical storms that have scuppered the wedding 'package'
they have equally trustingly bought into – is based on a pair of
squabbling holiday-makers spotted in Deia.

Storm Damage was published in 1988. Its title came partly from
the extraordinary storms that had swept unexpectedly across
Britain in the autumn of the previous year, but partly also from
Patten's own somewhat careworn state at that point. He had
emerged from a series of relationships – some serious, some less
so – feeling bruised and rather dissatisfied. He had turned 40 –

the ominous 'half-way through what time is left' point specified in 'Going Back and Going On'. His health had not been good. In the circumstances, it is perhaps unsurprising that the volume, when finally it emerged, proved something of a disappointment – not least to Patten himself, who almost immediately regretted its publication:

> During the time I was putting together the manuscript for *Storm Damage* I was going through a pretty disoriented period of my life. I wasn't happy, I wasn't well. I let a lot of poems go into the collection without working on them, and there are others I should have scrapped.

Despite the presence of a series of humorous poems (of rather mixed success, it has to be said) the overall atmosphere of *Storm Damage* is fairly bleak. A number of the poems, for example, show an acute and painful awareness of the passing of time. There is an atmosphere of nostalgia, of uncomfortable resignation, of missed opportunities. 'Going to Dinner' questions whether couples with children might regard a single male friend joining a dinner party as someone to be pitied, and reflects on what domestic bliss might possibly have been sacrificed for the sake of 'tenuous freedom'. Here, as at other points in the collection, Patten rescues a piece of potentially gloomy introspection by defusing the situation with humour. The poem gives itself a brisk talking-to and reminds itself that other people are less interested in our personal neuroses than we imagine:

> Yet perhaps I give that dinner too much weight.
> Perhaps for them
> The major drawback of the single man
> Is that he buggers up the seating plan.

Similarly, 'Where Are All Those Long-Haired Optimists Now?' shies away from an over-serious examination of failed dreams, contenting itself merely with fantasizing surrealistically that barbers are now 'standing over their graves, gloating'. A different kind of 'scissor-man' is here in operation, shearing locks of youthful hair and scything aspirations down to burial point.

Of the poems concerned with the past in *Storm Damage*, 'Looking Back On It (Again)' is a particularly interesting and in some ways rather poignant example. In this poem the juxtaposition of past and present is both graphic and real. The italicized first two stanzas appeared originally twenty-one years earlier as the poem 'Looking Back On It', written by Patten's teenage self and published in *Little Johnny's Confession*. The second two stanzas therefore function both as a commentary on the earlier poem and as a sequel to it:

> *At nineteen I was a brave old hunchback,*
> *Climbing to tremendous heights,*
> *Preparing to swing down on my golden rope*
> *And rescue Accused Innocence.*
>
> *But on my swooping, downward path one day*
> *Innocence ducked,*
> *And I amazed at such an act*
> *Crashed into a wall she had been building.*
>
> Twenty-one years later,
> Sitting stunned beside the same brick wall
> I see others climbing their golden ropes
> And hear Innocence sniggering.
>
> I say nothing much,
> But sit with bandages and the hope
> That maybe after all
> Some sweet fool might in time
> Swing right through that wall.

Again, the situation is tempered by humour and is ultimately void of self pity. The crash-landed Quasimodo figure is older and more knowing, but still loitering – albeit seated now, and quieter – beside the same wall. He is 'stunned' and swathed in bandages, but still harbours hopes that some 'sweet fool' may be luckier than himself. He may, for now, have put to one side his 'golden rope', but he has not limped away from the scene. The fantasy may yet become reality – and 'Salvage Operation', with its metaphor of deep-sea diving, also urges the importance of not consigning dreams to an unsalvageable abyss:

> Dive again, dreamer,
> Back down into the currents of the mutable self
> Where all that was lost might still drift,
> Battered, but salvageable.

'The Ambush' follows a similar pattern. It was written initially for a friend of Patten's, prone to catastrophes in love and now lamenting a further failed relationship. It begins with a gentle reminder of the need to keep grief of this nature in proportion. The immediate intensity of despair, it implies, will inevitably pass:

> When the face you swore never to forget
> Can no longer be remembered...

Ultimately, however, for all its wry humour, the poem is affirmative. It expresses Patten's continued conviction that love and hope will always resurface as human instincts too powerful to suppress, no matter how exhausting or dispiriting the consequent exposure to potential disappointment may prove to be:

> Emotions you thought had been put aside
> Will flare up within you and bleed you of reason.
> The routines which comforted you,
> And the habits in which you sought refuge
> Will bend like sunlight under water,
> And go astray.
> Your body will become a banquet,
> Falling heavenwards.
> You will loll in spring's sweet avalanche
> Without the burden of memory,
> And once again
> Monstrous love will swallow you.

Love may well be 'monstrous' in its all-engulfing enormity. But what else, the poem asks implicitly, can turn people's lives so completely and joyfully upside down that they are 'falling heavenwards'?

The sensuousness of 'The Ambush' – its image of a body to be feasted upon and its evocation of the wonderful decadence of languishing in an abundance of scented petals – links it clearly with some of Patten's earlier love poetry and demonstrates his continued control of this genre. In general, however, it seems fair to say that both *Grave Gossip* and *Storm Damage* are in retrospect chiefly significant because they took Patten into new territory. In *Grave Gossip*, he embarked on a serious contemplation of death. In *Storm Damage*, this preoccupation was continued to some extent – particularly in the evocative poem 'Her Father Rode a Horse Called Death' and in the fine 'Old

Ladies in the Churchyard', which was written in the churchyard at Ashprington, near Sharpham. But Patten also began in *Storm Damage* consciously to look backwards, from the perspective of early middle age, to the time of his own youth and the youth of his contemporaries. He began to seek to make sense of the larger patterns that were only now becoming visible across the distance.

In spring 1989, on tour in Australia following the publication of *Storm Damage*, Patten was interviewed in the newspaper *The Age* and made what was to be a prophetic remark about how these two concerns – a confronting of death and a confronting of his own past – might one day come together:

> I'm getting to the point where I want to explore the past, perhaps because I have started to smell the grave. I have only just realised that I can write about my childhood and I may make it my next book.

The 'next book' he had in mind at the time was a prose work, not yet completed. But in 1996 – prompted in part by the death of his mother in 1994 – 'the grave' and his childhood were indeed to become the dominant themes of *Armada*, his seventh and most recent poetry collection for adults and his finest work to date.

5

Going Back and Going On: Poems 1996

> going back
> Is just another way of going on.
> ('Going Back and Going On', *Grave Gossip / Grinning Jack*)

ARMADA

Patten's personal misgivings about the overall quality of *Storm Damage* made him reluctant to rush into writing a successor. In the years immediately following its publication, he was in any case extremely busy consolidating his growing reputation as a children's writer. His children's poetry collection *Gargling with Jelly* (published in 1985) had sold 200,000 copies, and he had been invited to edit *The Puffin Book of Twentieth-Century Children's Verse* – which appeared in 1991 to considerable critical acclaim (see Afterword, page 79). *Thawing Frozen Frogs*, his sequel to *Gargling with Jelly*, was also written over this period along with a range of children's story books. At the same time, he was touring widely – more often than not to places dogged by civil wars, as it turned out. In the Sudan, he read at the Islamic Students' Union in Khartoum. Later, as Yugoslavia began to disintegrate, he was in Macedonia. (Both visits resulted in poems later published in *Armada*.) Back in London, he continued to live in Brook Green – although he also spent several periods of 'quiet time' in the small fishing village of Mousehole, in Cornwall.

By the beginning to 1994 he was beginning to assemble a number of new poems. At that point the subjects were quite varied, although some (which were later published in the

'Between Harbours' section of *Armada*) concerned a difficult and obsessional love affair – soon to end – that had much preoccupied him over that winter. Then in March 1994 came a turning-point. His mother, Stella Bevan, suffered a brain haemorrhage – ironically, at the social club that had taken over the premises of the old Magnet cinema where Patten had spent so many hours of happy escapism as a child (see chapter 1, page 2). Patten hurried to her bedside in Liverpool, but she never regained consciousness. She died early in the morning of 13 March.

The death of his mother was very unexpected and painful. However, it was to inspire an extraordinarily rich and intense period of creativity, as Patten grieved for her, recalled his own childhood with her and sought to give meaning and permanence through his writing to both her living and her dying. The poems written in the months following her death – mostly grouped in the collection's first section ('The Armada') – are not only among the strongest in the collection as a whole but are undoubtedly among the best in his career. In its moving exploration of themes of adult suffering, of childhood memory and of human loss *Armada* becomes a memorial not only to Stella Bevan but also, by extension, to the countless people like her whose lives and deaths would normally go unremarked other than within their immediate community.

'Song of the Grateful Char', in *Grave Gossip* and *Grinning Jack*, had ended:

> There are many kinds of poverty,
> My mother knows them well.
> She sits and counts them in a tenement
> A mile or so from hell.

Stella Bevan's life – like the lives of most of those around her – had been one of hardship and of constant struggle with adversity, and the opening poem of *Armada* is almost unbearably poignant in its recognition of this:

> You never went to the ball, ever.
> In all your years sweeping kitchens
> No fairy godmother appeared, never.
>
> Poor, poor sweetheart,
> This rough white cloth, fresh from the hospital laundry,
> Is the only theatre-gown you've ever worn.

65

No make-up. Hair matted with sweat.
The drip beside your bed discontinued.
Life was never a fairy-tale.

Cinders soon.

('Cinders')

The mother's body lies still on the bed, almost suggesting – within the poem's framework of association – a tableau from *The Sleeping Beauty*. But the sleeping 'sweetheart' will never awaken. Tenderly the poem gives an imagined glimpse of her as a young girl, a Cinderella-figure 'sweeping kitchens' and dreaming of a handsome prince who would rescue her from drudgery and spirit her away to a world of society balls and theatres, of glamour and excitement. But the solemn sequence of 'never's tolls out the impossibility of the dream. At the close of the poem, the earlier image of youthful hope melts into the reality of the now-dead face and a woman as deprived in death – no make-up, no drip – as she was in life. And the harrowing last line provides the final cruel twist to the fairy tale that never happened – the reminder that the dream will soon literally come to ashes.

The second poem, 'The Armada', also begins with an echo of a fairy story – 'Long long ago'. But this 'long long ago' becomes not a mythical time of princes and princesses but the 'forty' years that separate the poet and his dead mother from their younger selves. Patten recalls himself as a 5-year-old, playing with a fleet of little ships made from paper and twigs:

> I stretched, belly-down on the grass beside a pond
> and to the far bank launched a child's armada.

The child's absorption in his game is total, as one by one his ships all come 'to ruin' and are 'on flame' in the pool red with sunset. It is only the adult son, looking back, who is now able to see the mother standing behind him – bored and shivering, but still allowing the child to play on:

> And you mother, stood behind me,
> impatient to be going,
> old at twenty-three, alone,
> thin overcoat flapping.

The image is ineffably sad. The young woman trapped into motherhood while still a girl herself is now 'old at twenty-three' and – as the commas emphasize by isolating her physically – dreadfully 'alone'. The 'thin overcoat flapping' gives in three words a fragile picture of poverty, vulnerability and oppression. The shifting of perspectives to achieve the richness of compassion that characterized earlier poetry such as 'You Come To Me Quiet As Rain Not Yet Fallen' (see chapter 3, pages 39–40) is here brought to perfection. The poem returns to the present, to 'the hospital a mile or so from that pond' where the mother lies dead. Memory and reality merge physically together. The mother's skin is as 'cool' as the surface of the pond all those years ago, and the gusts of wind that made her coat flutter and that blew away the child's sailing boats have now carried her forever out of reach of the son kneeling at her bedside:

> for as on a pond a child's paper boat
> was blown out of reach
> by the smallest gust of wind,
> so too have you been blown out of reach
> by the smallest whisper of death,
> and a childhood memory is sharpened,
> and the heart burns as that armada burnt,
> long, long ago.

'Long, long ago' is a major theme of *Armada*. In part the collection becomes not only a testament to a person but also a testament to a way of life now left behind – a Liverpool of gas lamps and waste lands, a childhood of paper boats and nightlights, an environment of backstreets busy with public happenings and private traumas. In 'The Betrayal' Patten reflects on the ease with which whole sections of history – private and public – can go unrecorded, and regrets what he describes as his own 'betrayal' in not having given sufficient attention to regarding or documenting the lives of the people among whom he grew up:

> There was so much I ought to have recorded,
> So many lives that have vanished –
> Families, neighbours; people whose pockets
> Were worn thin by hope. They were
> The loose change history spent without caring.
> Now they have become the air I breathe,
> Not to have marked their passing seems such a betrayal.

Unselfconsciously and without self-aggrandisement, 'The Betrayal' accepts Patten's public responsibility as sole survivor of his own background to speak out for a group of people that would otherwise have had no voice, and to give a record to a way of life that would otherwise simply vanish:

> What those who shaped me could not articulate
> Still howls for recognition as a century closes,
> And their homes are pulled down and replaced,
> And their backgrounds are wiped from the face of the earth.

Armada celebrates and gives dignity to ordinary lives – especially movingly so in 'So Many Different Lengths of Time', which is placed near the close of the collection as its summative and most authoritative statement on the theme of bereavement. It is framed as an answer to the question 'How Long is a Man's Life?' posed in a poem of the same title by the great Chilean poet Pablo Neruda (1904–1973), with whom Patten had read in 1972 (see chapter 1, page 11) and whose work he had found inspirational. The first two stanzas of 'So Many Different Lengths of Time' are a translation – done for Patten by Robert Graves's daughter, Lucia – of the first six lines of Neruda's poem, and the first four lines of the original are also printed in Spanish as the poem's epigraph. The device is highly effective. It serves immediately to take the poem into a universal context that is not defined by any one language or culture. Moreover, it also allows the poem itself to become an embodiment of its own answer to Neruda's question. People will live on for 'many different lengths of time', the poem affirms, within the lives and the thoughts of all of the people who remember them. A single life perpetuated in the memory of many different people therefore becomes multiple in its length. In the same way, Patten's poem is only one example of the countless future 'lives' that Neruda's poem will have.

'So Many Different Lengths of Time' is a great poem – transcendent in its psalm-like purity of language, in its compassion for the 'baffled' suffering of all mourners and in its triumphant affirmation of the ultimate value of every person's life, however humble. (Interestingly, it had already gained a significant public following even before its publication in *Armada*. Routinely after public readings and radio broadcasts of the poem, Patten had received – and agreed – many requests for permission for it to be read at funerals.) All people, the poem argues, are defined best by the friends and family they are closest to. It is the small shared details of individual daily lives that ultimately make people memorable to those who live on after them:

> A man lives for as long as we carry him inside us,
> for as long as we carry the harvest of his dreams,
> for as long as we ourselves live,
> holding memories in common, a man lives.

> His lover will carry his man's scent, his touch;
> his children will carry the weight of his love.
> One friend will carry his arguments,
> another will hum his favourite tunes,
> another will still share his terrors.

The theme of memory in *Armada* also has another very significant dimension, which is at once both more personal and equally general. As the quotation at the end of chapter 4 indicated (page 63), Patten was becoming increasingly aware that the leaving of Liverpool had not meant the leaving behind of his childhood. This remained as a part of his life that was still in many ways unexplored and unresolved. Now, revisiting memories of his childhood in *Armada*, he addresses for almost the first time since 'Johnny Learns the Language' (see chapter 3, page 34–5) the ways in which his own past continued to impact upon his present, and also considers more generally how people can prevent their childhood from being allowed to dictate their adulthood. Again, this is a successful new development in *Armada*, with Patten now achieving through contemplation of his own childhood the same translation of personal experience into universal terms that characterizes his love poetry. Moreover, in locating and defining the patterns between past and present that at first seem inescapable, the poems begin paradoxically – by their very existence – to suggest the possibilities of breaking free of such patterns. Once the unsayable has been said, it loses some of its terrors. Once a pattern has been fixed in time and space by a poem, it need not necessarily be repeated. It can sometimes be left on its page. 'Going back' – to quote the poem cited as the title of this chapter – can therefore become a way of 'going on'.

The death of Patten's mother was partly a liberation in this respect. Some areas of his past would inevitably have been difficult to explore previously, particularly in print. In 'Ghost Ship', for example, he confronts for the first time his feelings about his natural father, who had barely been mentioned during his childhood. Patten had known only that he was a merchant seaman. Then, unexpectedly, in 1991 his mother had confided that her reason for leaving him had been the chance discovery that two other women had also had children by him at around the time of Patten's birth. In 'Ghost Ship' these two pieces of information now come together, in the wake of his mother's death. In a poem of quite exquisite lyrical beauty (its shape outlining the silhouette of a ship's sails, rather as George Herbert's famous Metaphysical poem 'Easter Wings' was laid out to resemble a pair of angel wings), Patten reflects wistfully but stoically on the tide-turning consequences of 'fate and chance meetings' and bids an indirect farewell to the sailor father he never knew:

Dear ghost-ship,
since you left this port,
your young crew hot with longings,
their semen hardly dry on women's lips,
the years have shrunk to a single
fleck-foamed wave;
the one who fathered me,
long dead.

Though there is a harbour into which
it is best never to find the way,
a sea-route it is best
never to follow,
fate and chance meetings will always
undo reason.
It is the seal's breath
melts the ice floe,
the flip of a gull's wing
changes the wind's course.

'Stepfather' is a further poem that it would have been difficult for Patten to publish in his mother's lifetime, reconfirming as it does his continued inability to mourn the brutal stepfather who had by this point been dead for several years. What the poem does mourn is the 'what might have been| Had he not been' – by implication the happier life that both Patten's mother and Patten himself might have had, had they not been exposed to his stepfather's violence. The end of the poem gruesomely pictures him in his coffin, still exercising a malevolent power from beyond the grave:

> In the coffin he seems a replica,
> a terrible dummy,
>
> still wreaking havoc,
> still beating up the living.

The potential power of the dead over the living is explored at a number of points in *Armada*, most memorably in 'Echoes' (mentioned earlier, in chapter 1, pages 1–2), where Patten recalls the fierce independence of his crippled grandmother and her inability to break the shackles of her own pain to give or receive affection. Her iron callipers had become the spiritual 'ball and chain' within which she was imprisoned and with which she was in turn to imprison her family:

> She rejects all help, all love as I
> In later years will learn to do.
> Five years old. I cower from her authority.
> Clunk. Clunk. Clunk.
> The sound echoes through my history,
> And imprisons me.

In 'The Sick Equation', however, Patten challenges forcefully whether it is inevitable that errors will pass unchallenged from one generation to the next – a theory that famously led Larkin in 'This Be The Verse' to the wry conclusion 'And don't have any kids yourself'. Patten's poem describes the 'raw cocoon of parental hate' that caused his miserable childhood self to disbelieve the arithmetic of 'one and one made two' that he was taught at school and to resolve to stay well clear of all forms of addition in the future:

> I came to believe how it was best
> That one remained one,
> For by becoming two, one at least would suffer so.

Yet at the end of the poem he acknowledges that this was mistaken:

71

I was wrong of course,
Just as those who brought me up were wrong.
It's absurd to believe all others are as damaged as ourselves,
And however late on, I am better off for knowing now
That given love, by taking love all can in time refute
The lesson that our parents taught,
And in their sick equation not stay caught.

The final couplet here is arguably rather clumsy. 'The Sick Equation' is not among the strongest of Patten's *Armada* poems in technical terms. Its message, however, is of key importance to the collection as a whole. The destructive power of an unhappy childhood can be brought to an end, *Armada* suggests, if one returns to remembered situations – however painful they may be – in order to confront them as an adult. It is dangerous merely to accept and carry forward as unquestionable the impressions or assumptions that we may have formed as children. 'The Betrayal', for example, acknowledges from the perspective of an adult the extent of Patten's grandmother's suffering:

And my grandmother's hands!
Though I saw those poor, sleeping hands
Opening and closing like talons,
I did not see the grief they were grasping.

To the frightened child, the old red-nailed crippled woman had the appearance – and thus perhaps even the assumed evil powers – of a witch. The adult, however, can recognize the poor, sad human being who had no magic powers at all over someone else's future – nor even the power to cope with her own. The spell of the past is therefore broken.

'Inattention' contrasts very effectively the separate worlds of the adult and the child, although interestingly both the adult and the child in the poem are guilty in their separate ways of 'inattention' to each other. The child sits alone on the doorstep, lost first in a book filled with magical images of sea-going and then in his day-dreams of captaining a cargo ship. He is unaware of the encroachment of the real world. The shadow of the gasometer on the waste land across the street creeps across the poem – a 'slow irrevocable flood', not of ocean but of urban darkness. He is unaware even of what is going on in the next room. A woman is writing a letter of farewell, and packing belongings. Yet the reality, for the child, is the fantasy:

> Out on an ocean phosphite clings to rusting propellers,
> whales rise like islands, rain falls into nothing.

The child's world is compelling, its images hypnotic and alluring. But ultimately it is not real, and his faith in it will leave him painfully vulnerable. 'Inattention' derives considerable effect from the sparseness and ambiguity of narrative detail (Is the woman the child's mother? Is she leaving him or taking him with her?). The reader wonders what will happen next – but instinctively fears for the child.

'Inattention' – with its reference to 'cargo' and to sailing out on the ocean – is one of many poems in this collection that draw memorably on images of the sea. This is particularly true of the first section ('The Armada'), where nautical allusions include the paper boats of the title poem, the imagined 'cabin-boy' in 'The Eavesdropper', the crew of sailors in 'Ghost Ship' and the disturbing image of human shipwreck that prefaces 'Ward Sixteen':

> There was no sound other than the wheeze and creak of human
> wreckage,
> of souls adrift in a drugged sleep, clinging still to bodies washed
> by tidal-waves of pain.

The sea is also a presence in *Armada*'s other two sections, however. The second section is itself titled 'Between Harbours'. The third section includes 'Sea Saw' with its story of sailors whose hearts were 'cauterised by salt', as well as the peaceful exuberance of the leaping dolphins in 'Into the Blue' and the 'numbed bee' sailing with its 'cargo' through 'floating lakes of light' in the celebratory 'Full Circle World'. Moreover, 'Why Things Remained the Same' is prefaced by an epigraph translated from the Roman poet Horace: 'They change their sky, not their soul, who run across the sea.'

This sea imagery lends a powerful sense of continuity – as well as a special atmosphere of journeying – to *Armada* as a whole. In a collection that is in many ways concerned with journeys into the unknown, the sea itself not only becomes a metaphor for human experience, but also suggests a further world, as yet undiscovered, beyond that horizon. The collection's title is also of relevance in this respect, as Patten has explained:

> It was suggested to me that calling the book *Armada* might lead

people to think it was something to do with the Spanish Armada. The title poem '*The* Armada' does refer to ships, of course – or rather to the paper boats I made as a child. But words are not static. They can be made to evolve or, like magnets, attract new interpretations. Without the prefix 'A' or 'The' in the book's title, the word can be given a new resonance. It can be defamiliarised and opened up. At the moment of death, in the micro-second between being and non-being, perhaps consciousness enters a state that can be called *armada*, in which all an individual's million fragments of memory, all thoughts, all sensations simultaneously weigh anchor and set sail across unknowable space and time.

By the close of *Armada*, Patten himself has both weighed anchor and set sail. The past that had in some ways encumbered him – the 'weight of the baggage I carried' in 'Why Things Remained the Same' – has been explored, re-evaluated and contained. The debt to his background has been discharged. Like the butterfly in 'Survivor', both the poet and his lyric gift have triumphantly weathered the storm that cast its shadow over *Storm Damage*:

> Coming out of the storm it surprised us,
> A survivor, alighting on a snapped branch,
> Its wings still with their blue, crocus-coloured dust.

Armada has shown a poet wholly assured both of his purpose and of his direction in this collection. 'In Perspective', near the close of the volume, finds Patten ready now for the challenge of new experiences:

> Across the rich earth, the fat orchards, the fields I hardly knew,
> Happiness came bounding towards me,
> A hungry puppy, mistaking me for its master.
>
> Fine, I thought, let the mistake stand,
> The bones in my pockets
> Have weighed me down long enough.
>
> Happiness like sorrow, needs to be fed.

Afterword:
Writing for Children

CHILDREN'S FICTION

Patten's first book for children, *The Elephant and the Flower*, was inspired by a toy elephant that he fished out of the River Dart and which still resides in his back garden. (His children's play *The Pig and the Junkle* likewise had an object as a stimulus – this time a rusty robot found on a Liverpool rubbish tip, which he also still has.)

The Elephant and the Flower was published in 1970, and was to be the first of the many highly successful books that Patten was to write in his parallel career as a children's author. His move into children's writing was particularly timely at that point. It immediately provided him with a new dimension for further exploring some of the themes of childhood, magic and imagination that had preoccupied him in *Little Johnny's Confession* and *Notes to the Hurrying Man*. In some ways, perhaps, it became a partial solution to the problem identified in 'Ah Johnny, What When You're Older?' of how to buy a 'single back to innocence'. It also served as an important balance to the intensity of his adult writing. In an interview with the *Daily Telegraph* magazine in 1990, Patten described writing for children as taking 'a holiday from one's own seriousness'.

Patten's fiction for children ranges from the fabulous to the urban and contemporary, and – although all of his children's writing contains humour – his tone can also vary from the quietly serious to the broadly comic. At one extreme is the enchanting fable *Jumping Mouse*, for example (referred to in Chapter 4, page 57 and now printed in *Grizzelda Frizzle and Other*

Stories) which is derived from a Navajo Indian folk tale. Described by Charles Causley in *Twentieth Century Children's Writers* as 'a small masterpiece', it is set in a world of talking animals and of magic, and is told in the timeless heightened language of fairy stories:

> In the roots of a giant tree there once lived a family of mice. It was a huge family, and they lived in semi-darkness, for the tree's thick branches hid the sunlight from them, and they went about their business hardly ever venturing out into the world...

At the other extreme, a story such as *Impossible Parents* (1994) is entirely modern in its setting and diction. It offers cheerful knockabout comedy, with Ben and Mary suffering agonies of shame at the antics of their relentlessly embarrassing parents – complete with pony tail and nose-ring (dad) and fishnet body-stocking (mum).

Impossible Parents is quite unusual among Patten's stories for children in that the story remains located throughout the book in the 'real' world – albeit an exuberantly anarchic version of reality. More usually in Patten's children's fiction, the world of magic will also be introduced to intervene in or intermingle with the humdrum world of ordinary life. The story 'Grizzelda Frizzle', for example, is set among the dilapidated tower blocks of the Thumbledown Estate but includes a heroine with 'a teeny-weeny bit of witch's blood' and a prince who turns into a frog. Characteristically in Patten's writing for children, the real and the magical come together – very much as they did in his earlier poetry for adults – and this balance is central not only to the special atmosphere of the writing but also ultimately to its meaning. In an interview quoted in the most recent entry on his writing in volume 43 of *Contemporary Authors: New Revision Series* ed. Susan M. Trotsky (Gale Research Inc. 1994), Patten explained the reasons behind this approach:

> I am interested in fantasy, but always set the fantastic against realistic backgrounds, so that the everyday world is put into a different perspective. I feel that this combination helps to develop the imagination. It is also a way of commenting on our hopes and fears. 'Reality' is not constant. Each child and adult creates his own version of it, depending on his needs. (p. 359)

Perhaps the most outstanding success in this fusion of fantasy and realism is one of Patten's best-known works for children – the novel *Mr Moon's Last Case* (1975), which received a special award in 1977 from the Mystery Writers of America Guild. It tells the story of a retired policeman (Mr Moon) and his pursuit of a dwarf (Nameon) who is trying to return to his own world, and it brings together the two genres of fairy tale and detective story within a narrative that is rich in allusion and atmosphere.

Part of the special atmosphere of *Mr Moon's Last Case* derives from images and scenes remembered from Patten's own childhood. Indeed, the novel's central situation was triggered by a Liverpool memory. In July 1964, a young Liverpool boy had told a group of friends that he had seen a leprechaun in the city's Jubilee Park, setting in motion a rumour that was to lead to a stampede of over 2,000 schoolchildren converging on the park in search of the leprechaun. The mayhem that resulted had the St John's Ambulance Brigade out in force. In Patten's novel, the dwarf Nameon – described as 'a creature resembling a leprechaun' – is real not imaginary, but the excitement generated among humans by his presence draws on Patten's amused recollection of the hysteria that had overtaken Liverpool's children eleven years earlier.

The settings in *Mr Moon's Last Case* are varied, since the story takes the form of a chase. Unsurprisingly, however, Liverpool features quite prominently as the fictional 'Steelborough' (complete with a Magnet cinema); and the atmosphere of the book as a whole is gently evocative of the fifties or early sixties, as Patten noted himself in an interview published in the *Liverpool Echo* in 1975:

> There's lots of fragments of my own childhood in the book...an air of gaslit early fifties streets.

Similarly, as he pointed out in the same interview, a number of individual characters in the story were drawn from people that Patten had encountered in his childhood. For instance, Mr O' Lovelife, a strange old tramp in a battered tailcoat, was based on a very particular memory of a Liverpool street singer:

> I remember as a child, on kind of rainy Sundays, an old man coming walking down the streets singing 'If I were a blackbird I'd whistle and sing' and we used to run out and give him some money.

Interestingly, however, by no means all of the locations in *Mr Moon's Last Case* are drawn directly from childhood experience. For instance, 'Norton Bay' is based on the town of Seaton Carew in the north-east of England, which had been in the news in January 1974 because a freak tide had been expected to uncover the prehistoric forests beneath its 4,000-year-old coastal peat beds. 'Norton Bay' therefore became Patten's chosen site for the intersection between the modern world and Nameon's forest home – and it is here, at the end of the novel, that the wrecked lifeboat that first brought him into the human world magically reappears. (The *Northern Echo* of 12 January 1974 reported a number of recent archaeological finds at Seaton Carew, including part of a wrecked sailing ship. Patten still has his copy of the newspaper, and against the description of the wrecked ship he has written 'Nameon's boat'.)

Mr Moon's Last Case has been described by many reviewers as a potential classic, and it is clearly impossible to do justice to it in a brief Afterword note. In summary, however, its appeal – like that of the very best of children's fiction – can be seen to operate on many different levels. On a straightforward level, its narrative has the energy, humour and suspense to capture a child's imagination. More subtly, its characters are thoughtfully and compassionately developed – with adult readers in particular drawn to the sensitive portrayal of Mr Moon: old, ill and tired but utterly dogged and dauntless in his firm belief in a world beyond his own. But, above all, the story is written with a lyrical precision that makes it unmistakably and triumphantly the work of a poet, as Margery Fisher stressed in a review in *Growing Point* in 1975:

> The interlocking worlds of imagination and discovery are pictorialised in prose which can be terse or musical, melancholy or comic, but which is always exact and reverberant.

CHILDREN'S POETRY

Writing poetry for children came rather later to Patten than writing children's fiction. His first book of children's verse – *Gargling with Jelly* – did not appear until 1985, although its success (as noted in chapter 5, page 64) was immediate and spectacular. *Thawing Frozen Frogs*, which followed in 1990, has also achieved immense popularity.

In his Introduction to *The Puffin Book of Twentieth-Century Children's Verse* which he edited in 1991 – and which received considerable critical recognition for its innovative selection of poems and the use of reverse chronology in the ordering of contributors – Patten expressed his belief that children's poetry can often survive the passing of time with a greater immediacy than adult poetry:

> poems written for children retain their freshness. The best have a sense of wonder, mystery and mischief that their older brothers and sisters often seem to lose. (p. 19)

This genuine respect for the genre is at the heart of Patten's success as a children's poet. He has never underestimated the skill involved in writing poetry for children. In an interview in the *Independent* in 1992 he commented:

> You're not talking about the difference between playing with language or touching on emotions or delving much more deeply. Writing for children requires a totally different form, and is technically much more exacting.

Accordingly, his poetry is no less crafted for having been written for a school-age readership. And his sensitivity to his young audiences translates into poetry that demonstrates an instinctive understanding of what appeals to and preoccupies children. Interviewed in the Australian newspaper *The Age* in 1989, he said, 'Every syllable has got to be right for kids. You owe it to them to do it very well'.

Humour, unsurprisingly, is an important element – ranging from anarchic puns (grown-ups are 'groan-ups', for instance) to a Dahl-like delight in the grotesque and/or disgusting. Poems such as 'Pick-a-Nose Pick' in *Gargling With Jelly* have prompted a number of parental protests to schools and libraries on taste grounds, but are absolutely in tune with their young readers' intuitive love of rhyme, rhythm and 'naughty' words ('Pick-a-Nose Pick' has now, in fact, become a playground skipping game). Many of the comic poems – such as 'Cousin Lesley's See-Through Stomach' from *Gargling With Jelly* – have a domestic context, and introduce eccentric family members (Patten's most recent children's poetry book – *The Utter Nutters*, published in

1995 – presents an entire street full of weirdos and eccentrics). Others – such as 'How The New Teacher Got Her Nickname' from *Thawing Frozen Frogs* – have a school setting. But the effect is always entertainingly subversive. The child can recognize the familiar setting, but be thrilled by the (usually anti-authoritarian) way in which the familiar is then transformed.

'Mischief' – which he identified in the Introduction to *The Puffin Book of Twentieth-Century Children's Verse* (quoted above) as an important element of children's poetry – is rife in Patten's poems for children. They brim with energy and fun. But, significantly, his collections also range more widely, touching sometimes on issues such as death or divorce ('Looking For Dad' from *Gargling With Jelly* is an example of the latter) and also achieving in a number of the more thoughtful or serious poems a memorable lyrical intensity that does indeed attain the 'sense of wonder' and 'mystery' that Patten also put forward as prerequisites for enduring success. A number of poems from *Gargling with Jelly* – 'The Apple-Flavoured Worm', 'The Bee's Last Journey to the Rose' and 'The Complaint' – were included three years later in the adult collection *Storm Damage*. And *Thawing Frozen Frogs* also includes a number of timeless lyrics of similar calibre – such as 'Spider Apples', 'Sally Slipshod' and the magical 'Hide-away Sam':

> Hide-away Sam sat in the darkness,
> Pale as the day he was born,
> A miser who stored up his blessings
> Yet looked on all blessings with scorn.
>
> He peeped through a chink in the doorway,
> A crack on which the sun shone.
> All the things he had craved danced past him,
> He blinked and they were gone.
>
> A ladder was stretched up to Heaven,
> Its rungs were covered with dew,
> At its foot was a bucket of diamonds
> (From the sky God had stolen a few)
>
> And beyond the ladder an orchard
> Where bees dunked in pollen flew
> Between the falling blossom
> And the core of a fruit that was new.

80

'Time to come out and enjoy life!'
A voice boomed down from above.
'Time to swap ten aeons of darkness
For one bright second of love.'

But Hide-away Sam shrank inwards.
He refused to open the door.
The Angel of Mercy lost patience,
Shrugged, and said no more.

Select Bibliography

The bibliography that follows is concerned solely with Patten's work for adults, since that has formed the basis of this study. However, the titles, dates of publication and publishers of his works for children are given in the Biographical Outline on pages xii-xiv.

WORKS BY BRIAN PATTEN FOR ADULTS (FIRST BRITISH EDITIONS)

Penguin Modern Poets No. 10: The Mersey Sound with Adrian Henri and Roger McGough (London: Penguin, 1967; revised edition, 1974).
Little Johnny's Confession (London: Allen and Unwin, 1967).
Notes to the Hurrying Man: Poems Winter '66 – Summer '68 (London: Allen and Unwin, 1969).
The Irrelevant Song and Other Poems (London: Allen and Unwin, 1971; revised edition, 1975).
Vanishing Trick (London: Allen and Unwin, 1976).
Grave Gossip (London: Allen and Unwin, 1979).
Love Poems (London: Allen and Unwin, 1981).
New Volume, with Adrian Henri and Roger McGough (London: Penguin, 1983).
Storm Damage (London: Unwin Hyman, 1988).
Grinning Jack: Selected Poems (London: Unwin Hyman, 1990).
Armada (London: HarperCollins, 1996).

The Note on the Texts on page xv clarifies the present position in relation to the availability of these texts. The above list includes all published work by Patten that is publicly available. However, a complete bibliography of his work for adults, including a range of small private editions of individual poems or groups of poems published in the 1970s, is given in *Contemporary Poets*, 5th edition, ed. Tracy Chevalier (London: St James Press, 1991).

RECORDINGS

Selections from Little Johnny's Confession and Notes to the Hurrying Man and New Poems (Caedmon, 1969). A solo reading.
Vanishing Trick (Tangent, 1976). Readings by Patten of poems from this collection, plus musical settings of some poems sung by Linda Thompson and Norma Winston.

BIOGRAPHICAL AND CRITICAL STUDIES

This is the first book-length consideration of Patten's work, and very little of substance has been published to date in relation to his work. However, the following texts were of assistance to me in preparing this study.

Booth, Martin, *British Poetry 1964–84: Driving Through the Barricades* (London: Routledge & Kegan Paul, 1985). An interesting and intelligent survey, including in the chapter 'The Lunatics, the Lovers and the Poets' a brief but sympathetic consideration of Patten's poetic development.
Causley, Charles, 'Brian Patten', *Twentieth Century Children's Writers*, 3rd edition, ed. Tracy Chevalier (London: St James Press, 1989). A brief but warm and positive evaluation of Patten's work as a writer for both adults and children.
Davie, Donald, 'Larkin's Choice', *Listener*, volume 89, no. 2296 (29. 3. 73). An attack on Patten's poem 'Portrait of a Young Girl Raped at a Suburban Party' which Philip Larkin included in his edition of *The Oxford Book of 20th Century English Verse* (Oxford: Oxford University Press, 1973).
Holbrook, David, *Lost Bearings in English Poetry* (London: Visions Press, 1977). The chapter 'Modern Poetry and the Death of Sympathy' includes negative criticism of Patten's work – focusing on 'Ode on Celestial Music' and 'Portrait of a Young Girl Raped at a Suburban Party' – and an unfavourable comparison with Thomas Hardy. His interpretation of 'Ode on Celestial Music', quite remarkably, misses the point of the poem entirely.

Horovitz, Michael (ed.) *Children of Albion* (London: Penguin, 1969). An anthology of so-called 'Underground' poetry. The work of the Liverpool Poets is omitted deliberately, since they were by that time already in print, but Horovitz's long (and at this point somewhat dated) essay at the end of the volume includes comment on their influence and importance.

Lindop, Grevel, 'Poetry, Rhetoric and the Mass Audience: The Case of the Liverpool Poets', *British Poetry Since 1960* ed. G. Lindop and M. Schmidt (London: Carcanet, 1972). A largely unsympathetic account of the Liverpool Poets' early work, particularly stressing its performance origins.

Lucie-Smith, Edward (ed.), *The Liverpool Scene* (London: Donald Carroll, 1967). An influential and interesting anthology of poems and photographs, including short interviews with Patten and other poets performing in Liverpool in the mid-sixties.

Melly, George, *Revolt Into Style: The Pop Arts in Britain* (London: Penguin, 1970). An entertaining study, containing only brief reference to Patten individually but providing a useful account of the period from a fellow-Liverpudlian.

Nuttall, Jeff, *Bomb Culture* (London: McGibbon & Kee, 1968). An analysis of youth culture in the sixties, particularly in the contexts of political protest and the arts. Nuttall suggests (p. 132) that Patten's work influenced the lyrics of the Beatles.

Porter, Peter, 'The Poet in the Sixties: Vices and Virtues', *British Poetry Since 1960*, ed. G. Lindop and M. Schmidt (London: Carcanet, 1972). The transcript of a recorded conversation, which includes a brusque dismissal of the works of the Liverpool Poets.

Thwaite, Anthony, *Poetry Today – A Critical Guide to British Poetry* (London: Longman, 1985). A readable general overview. The chapter 'Pop and After' makes brief reference to the Liverpool Poets.

Index

(Works are listed after their authors' names)

Recent and
Forthcoming Titles
in the
New Series of

WRITERS AND
THEIR WORK

WRITERS AND THEIR WORK

TITLES IN PREPARATION

Title	Author
Peter Ackroyd	*Susana Onega*
Kingsley Amis	*Richard Bradford*
Antony and Cleopatra	*Ken Parker*
Jane Austen	*Robert Clark*
Alan Ayckbourn	*Michael Holt*
J. G. Ballard	*Michel Delville*
Samuel Beckett	*Keir Elam*
William Blake	*John Beer*
Elizabeth Bowen	*Maud Ellmann*
Emily Brontë	*Stevie Davies*
S.T. Coleridge	*Stephen Bygrave*
Crime Fiction	*Martin Priestman*
Daniel Defoe	*Jim Rigney*
Charles Dickens	*Rod Mengham*
Carol Ann Duffy	*Deryn Rees Jones*
George Eliot	*Josephine McDonagh*
E.M. Forster	*Nicholas Royle*
Brian Friel	*Geraldine Higgins*
Henry IV	*Peter Bogdanov*
Henrik Ibsen	*Sally Ledger*
Kazuo Ishiguro	*Cynthia Wong*
Julius Caesar	*Mary Hamer*
Franz Kafka	*Michael Wood*
John Keats	*Kelvin Everest*
Rudyard Kipling	*Jan Montefiore*
Langland: *Piers Plowman*	*Claire Marshall*
D.H. Lawrence	*Linda Ruth Williams*
Measure for Measure	*Kate Chedgzoy*
William Morris	*Anne Janowitz*
Vladimir Nabokov	*Neil Cornwell*
Sylvia Plath	*Elizabeth Bronfen*
Alexander Pope	*Pat Rogers*
Dennis Potter	*Derek Paget*
Lord Rochester	*Peter Porter*
Christina Rossetti	*Kathryn Burlinson*
Salman Rushdie	*Damian Grant*
Sir Walter Scott	*John Sutherland*
Mary Shelley	*Catherine Sharrock*
P. B. Shelley	*Paul Hamilton*
Stevie Smith	*Alison Light*
Wole Soyinka	*Mpalive Msiska*
Laurence Sterne	*Manfred Pfister*
Jonathan Swift	*Claude Rawson*
The Tempest	*Gordon McMullan*
Dylan Thomas	*Graham Holderness*
Derek Walcott	*Stewart Brown*
Evelyn Waugh	*Malcolm Bradbury*
John Webster	*Thomas Sorge*
Mary Wollstonecraft	*Jane Moore*
William Wordsworth	*Nicholas Roe*
Working Class Fiction	*Ian Haywood*
W.B. Yeats	*Ed Larrissy*

JOHN CLARE
John Lucas

Setting out to recover Clare – whose work was demeaned and damaged by the forces of the literary establishment – as a great poet, John Lucas offers the reader the chance to see the life and work of John Clare, the 'peasant poet' from a new angle. His unique and detailed study portrays a knowing, articulate and radical poet and thinker writing as much out of a tradition of song as of poetry. This is a comprehensive and detailed account of the man and the artist which conveys a strong sense of the writer's social and historical context.

"Clare's unique greatness is asserted and proved in John Lucas's brilliant, sometimes moving, discourse." **Times Educational Supplement.**

John Lucas has written many books on nineteenth- and twentieth-century literature, and is himself a talented poet. He is Professor of English at Loughborough University.

0 7463 0729 2 paperback 96pp

GEORGE HERBERT
T.S. Eliot
With a new introductory essay by **Peter Porter**

Another valuable reissue from the original series, this important study – one of T. S. Eliot's last critical works – examines the writings of George Herbert, considered by Eliot to be one of the loveliest and most profound of English poets. The new essay by well-known poet and critic Peter Porter reassesses Eliot's study, as well as providing a new perspective on Herbert's work. Together, these critical analyses make an invaluable contribution to the available literature on this major English poet.

0 7463 0746 2 paperback 80pp £5.99

CHILDREN'S LITERATURE
Kimberley Reynolds

Children's literature has changed dramatically in the last hundred years and this book identifies and analyses the dominant genres which have evolved during this period. Drawing on a wide range of critical and cultural theories, Kimberley Reynolds looks at children's private reading, examines the relationship between the child reader and the adult writer, and draws some interesting conclusions about children's literature as a forum for shaping the next generation and as a safe place for developing writers' private fantasies.

"The book manages to cover a surprising amount of ground . . . without ever seeming perfunctory. It is a very useful book in an area where a short pithy introduction like this is badly needed." **Times Educational Supplement**

Kimberley Reynolds lectures in English and Women's Studies at Roehampton Institute, where she also runs the Children's Literature Research Unit.

0 7463 0728 4 paperback 112pp

LEO TOLSTOY
John Bayley

Leo Tolstoy's writing remains as lively, as fascinating, and as absorbing as ever and continues to have a profound influence on imaginative writing. This original and elegant study serves as an introduction to Tolstoy, concentrating on his two greatest novels – *War and Peace* and *Anna Karenina* – and the ancillary texts and tales that relate to them. By examining how Tolstoy created a uniquely spacious and complex fictional world, John Bayley provides a fascinating analysis of the novels, explaining why they continue to delight and inform readers today.

John Bayley is Warton Professor of English Emeritus at St Catherine's College, University of Oxford.

0 7463 0744 6 paperback 96pp

EDMUND SPENSER
Colin Burrow

Considered by many to be the greatest Elizabethan poet, Edmund Spenser's writing has inspired both admiration and bewilderment. The grace of Spenser's language and his skilful and enchanting evocation of the fairy world have, for many, been offset by the sheer bulk and complexity of his work. Colin Burrow's considered and highly readable account provides a reading of Spenser which clarifies the genres and conventions used by the writer. Burrow explores the poet's taste for archaism and allegory, his dual attraction to images of vital rebirth and mortal frailty, and his often conflictual relationship with his Queen and with the Irish landscape in which he spent his mature years.

Colin Burrow is Fellow, Tutor and College Lecturer in English at Gonville & Caius College, University of Cambridge.

0 7463 0750 0 paperback 128pp

HENRY FIELDING
Jenny Uglow

In this fresh introduction to his work, Uglow looks at Fielding in his own historical context and in the light of recent critical debates. She identifies and clarifies many of Fielding's central ideas, such as those of judgement, benevolence and mercy which became themes in his novels. Looking not only at the novels, but also at Fielding's drama, essays, journalism and political writings, Uglow traces the author's development, clarifies his ideas on his craft, and provides a fascinating insight into eighteenth-century politics and society.

Jenny Uglow is a critic and publisher.

0 7463 0751 9 paperback 96pp

HENRY JAMES
The Later Writing
Barbara Hardy

Barbara Hardy focuses on Henry James's later works, dating from 1900 to 1916. Offering new readings of the major novels and a re-evaluation of the criticism to date, she considers language and theme in a number of Jamesian works, including *The Ambassadors, The Wings of the Dove* and *The Golden Bowl,* and engages with his autobiographical and travel writing and literary criticism. Hardy's analysis traces two dominant themes – the social construction of character and the nature of creative imagination – and reveals James to be a disturbing analyst of inner life.

Barbara Hardy is Professor Emeritus at Birkbeck College, University of London.

0 7463 0748 9 paperback 96pp

DAVID LODGE
Bernard Bergonzi

Internationally celebrated as both a novelist and a literary critic, David Lodge is one of Britain's most successful and influential living writers. He has been instrumental in introducing and explaining modern literary theory to British readers while maintaining, in regard to his own work, "faith in the future of realistic fiction". Bergonzi's up-to-date and comprehensive study covers both Lodge's critical writing as well as his novels of the past 35 years (from *The Picturegoers* to *Therapy*) and explores how he expresses and convincingly combines metafiction, realism, theology and dazzling comedy.

Bernard Bergonzi is Emeritus Professor of English at the University of Warwick.

0 7463 0755 1 paperback 80pp

DAVID HARE
Jeremy Ridgman

David Hare is one of the most prolific, challenging, and culturally acclaimed playwrights in Britain today. Jeremy Ridgman's study focuses on the dramatic method that drives the complex moral and political narratives of Hare's work. He considers its relationship to its staging and performance, looking in particular at the dramatist's collaborations with director, designer, and performer. Hare's writing for the theatre since 1970 is set alongside his work for television and film and his achievements as director and translator, to provide a detailed insight into key areas of his dramatic technique particularly dialogue, narrative, and epic form.

Jeremy Ridgman is Senior Lecturer in the Department of Drama and Theatre Studies at Roehampton Institute, London

0 7463 0774 8 paperback 96pp